Create an Enduring
Legacy

The Essential, Simple Guide For
Creating Your Book In The Self - Publishing Market

Wayne Rollan Melton
and
Patty Atcheson Melton

"Create an Enduring Legacy
The Essential, Simple Guide For Creating Your Book
In The Self-Publishing Market"

Fix Bay Inc Publishing

Melton, Wayne Rollan
Atcheson-Melton, Patty

1. Business 2. Publishing 3. Books

ISBN: 978-0-9838149-5-5

*" "Don't look for me at my headstone,
but within the
covers of my book
long after I'm
gone from this earth. " "*
-Anonymous

Dedication

This book is dedicated to everyone determined
to leave an enduring legacy

Table of Contents

Chapter

1

Create an Enduring Legacy

Weeds grow at a ferocious rate just three blocks from our home at the heart of the American west. The overgrown vegetation covers or obscures literally hundreds of long-forgotten gravesites filled with pioneers who lived in the 1800s.

Thieves stole or broke many of the headstones over a period of decades. During more than a century since those funerals, harsh winters and dry summer winds gently carved away and obliterated most of the engravings—including names to dates.

Today in the 21st Century, like many of our neighbors we're unaware of any personal stories behind these long-buried individuals. Sadly, whenever we stroll past or drive near this fenced-off field, the scene forces us to face an unavoidable reality.

With just as much growing intensity, many of us crave and strive for our own so-called "15 minutes of fame" within this lifetime.

Every Memorial Day and Veterans Day we realize that not a single flower, wreath or banner has been left for the long-departed souls. Yes, these people once cried, laughed, and played in much the way that we all do—but now they've long since been forgotten.

On a recent spring day a lonely, hungry and skinny dog somehow managed to squirm through a hole in a chain-link fence that surrounds the site. Once inside, the dog wailed like a lonely coyote, as if crying out for the souls of those who never will be known during the 21st Century and beyond.

The Past Becomes a Puzzle

As the worldwide population whisks into the upper stratosphere of more than 7 billion souls, in a sense each of us evolves into a grain of sand upon a massive beach. Yes, for thousands of years virtually every society and culture has pondered the meaning of life.

Why are you here, and does your life have any meaning? Will the memory of you end up obliterated by the passage of time, like the dust that covers those many long-forgotten graves across the American West, in every state and nation?

"Don't look for me at my headstone, but within the covers of my book long after I'm gone from this earth," says an age-old anonymous quote.

10

This summarizes the inner fire that blazes within the hearts of today's most successful authors and book publishers, a chance for our descendants to remember us.

With just as much growing intensity, many of us crave and strive for our own so-called "15 minutes of fame" within this lifetime. We either want to bask in the media spotlight, or to teach the rest of the world about our lives, experiences, philosophies or discoveries.

"Look at me, because I have something to share!" many of us want to sing or say to the entire world. "Take notice of my real-life story, or my fictional tale, or maybe you can benefit from this essential 'how-to' information that only I can provide."

"Why would anyone want to listen to me, or to read my story? How does my opinion and knowledge matter at all?"

Appreciate, Acknowledge and Tell Your Own Story

"But I do not have a story to tell," some people might say, when given the opportunity to easily bring their message to the entire world. "Why would anyone want to listen to me, or to read my story? How does my opinion and knowledge matter at all?"

To the contrary, each of us has a crucial and urgent story to tell, everyone from college students to mature people living in advanced health care centers. By just being here, each of us

"This is your story, not ours. We only serve as your guides, your personal messengers in getting you onto a pathway where the world can appreciate your achievements, or learn the essential lessons that you can provide."

has been given the gift of life, everyone blessed as unique and vibrant.

Through the years at Fix Bay Inc Publishing and WOW! Design Marketing we have eagerly helped many people get their stories told. Lots of them now friends of ours, these diverse clients have ranged from little-known middle class individuals to world-renowned business and medical professionals.

Our vibrant cadre of clients includes everyone from a notorious robber who became a philanthropist, to a world-famous physician known for his vital medical discoveries. With just as much urgency, streams of everyday "unknown" individuals seek our vital experience in helping them to get the widespread recognition they richly deserve. Simply stated, our clients seek leadership and guidance in getting their stories told.

"Our job is to help you get the worldwide recognition that you richly deserve," we tell them. "This is your story, not ours. We only serve as your guides, your personal messengers in getting you onto a pathway where the world can appreciate your achievements, or learn the essential lessons that you can provide."

We Work Behind the Scenes to Get You Recognition

As you'll soon discover in the pages that follow, through many years of personal experience, continual learning and trying new techniques, we've become experts on the many ways that people can get their stories told.

Our vibrant and ever-growing processes range from the creation of low-cost but high-quality Websites and video production to the development, generation and production of various types of books. These range from what experts now call standard "dead-tree books" offered in stores and libraries, to eBooks sold online.

With humble grace, kindness, understanding and empathy, we're about to give you the basic "how-to" secrets—the best, most efficient ways to benefit from these various media. With our guidance and advice, in a flash you'll learn the essential secrets to getting on the fast track to worldwide recognition.

"In the future, everyone will be famous for 15 minutes," an American painter and film maker, Andrew Warhola Jr—better known as "Andy Warhol"—said in 1968. His often-used phrase soon stuck into the American vernacular.

Now more than four decades later, ever-advancing technology can make "15 minutes" possible for just about anyone. The trick is to look to experts such as us for guidance and suggestions on how to get such recognition fast and with great efficiency.

Until the late 1800s and early 1900s, the most efficient way for average Americans to chronicle their lives and experiences was to use ink pens to write on paper.

Everything Old is New Again

A hit song, "Everything Old is New Again" mesmerized the world in a runaway hit 1979 American musical film "All that Jazz," directed by legendary choreographer Bob Fosse. In essence, the tune tells us to live life to the fullest and celebrate because nothing truly ever changes.

Indeed, many of us embrace joys, hopes, dreams, desires and sorrows similar to those that long-forgotten pioneers experienced in the early American West. The only difference is that new technology improved communication, plus the storage and dissemination of data.

Until the late 1800s and early 1900s, the most efficient way for average Americans to chronicle their lives and experiences was to use ink pens to write on paper. Yet the vast majority of those documents eventually withered or were lost.

By contrast, today's digital technology enables even low income individuals to permanently memorialize their personal stories or knowledge via non-corroding, everlasting software.

"A lot of the time people don't really know what they want until you show it to them," Steve Jobs, founder and former CEO of Apple Computer told "Business Week" in 1998. Indeed, for anyone wanting to leave a legacy, the trick rests in understanding basic digital systems.

Technology Goes Beyond the Grave

Entrepreneurs shot today's technology into another stratosphere in 2011, by introducing a creative and unique way for dead people to "speak" to those of us visiting their graves. Word of this new strategy soon became a social media sensation.

Various monument companies began installing bar code scanning applications at the gravesites. Mourners or curious people strolling through cemeteries use this system to instantly access online obituaries or even "lifetime" videos featuring the now-departed.

"Isn't it strange that I who have written only popular books should be such a strange fellow?" said Albert Einstein, the world-renowned genius and scientist famous worldwide in the 20th Century. Could Einstein possibly have envisioned today's many media systems?

Lots of people who get mired in this proverbial whirlwind find themselves ensconced in the so-called "cult of celebrity." Few people can argue against the fact that the American culture gets caught up in our collective adulation of famous people.

At some point fame essentially begins to feed upon itself, occasionally reaching a point where certain untalented individuals become merely "famous for being famous." In sharp contrast, the

The public never realizes that we're the people driving the marketing and image machine.

systems that we use, recommend and embrace focus on facts, intriguing historical documentation and essential educational information that people can benefit from right away.

Celebrities Look to Us for Expertise

Rather than "dumbing down" their media strategies, our clients look to us to use the various media to help manage their images. Just as important, these clients including world-renowned celebrities appreciate the fact that we work "behind the scenes." The public never realizes that we're the people driving the marketing and image machine.

Embracing this strategy, a celebrity whom we have never worked with, Todd Solondz, an American independent screenwriter and director has been quoted as saying that, "Anonymity is very important to me, and I don't want to be recognized in public more than I already am."

Many of those whom we work with feel this way as well, while also remaining energized by the persistent need to regularly convey their stories, messages and images to the public.

Like us, most individuals in our continually growing list of clients recognize and appreciate the fact that overall the public has grown pessimistic, apathetic and even angered by mindless trivia prevalent in today's popular culture.

Caucasian rap music star and international entertainment sensation Eminem struck the proverbial nail on the head in this regard when he told the media: "Fame hit me on the head like a ton of bricks."

"Fame hit me on the head like a ton of bricks."

-Eminem

Fully cognizant of how such transitions can impact our clients' lives, we strive for well-reasoned, vibrant and cohesive media strategies to minimize such potential chaos.

Chapter

2

Strive to Achieve Success

in the Book World

Amid today's crazy, mind-numbing and relentless media maze, seemingly everyone seems to have his or her own book these days.

The relentless onslaught of so-called talking heads on 24-hour cable news channels, morning talk shows and daytime chat programs feature an endless parade of people labeled as "superstars" or expert analysts.

Invariably, a sharply increasing percentage of these guests have their own "latest and greatest" books to promote. These publications often get casually mentioned in passing, or become the primary focus of on-screen interviews.

Compounding this never-ending, relentless media maze, virtually all hosts of regularly scheduled TV programs and radio-talk shows each have their own books to pitch as well. Everyone from Oprah Winfrey to Bill O'Reilly of Fox News, talk-radio host Rush Limbaugh and countless others regularly release their own books as well.

But why do these celebrities feel a burning need to write, create and generate their own books? Why do virtually all of them undergo the arduous time, effort and expense necessary to pitch their own publications? And, why on earth do the various cable channels and program-syndication firms permit such shameless self-promotion?

The answers are multi-fold and essential for implementing an effective overall marketing strategy for any celebrity and for everyday "unknown" people as well.

Besides providing the potential for huge personal revenues, a well-written, compelling and timely book can create and legitimize a "celebrity" or "expert" in the public mindset.

Add to this the fact that we live in a gossip-oriented, fame-obsessed society where fame and fortune remain primary goals, and the motivations become crystal clear.

"The fact that 15 minutes of fame has extended a little longer than 15 minutes is somewhat surprising to me and completely baffling to my wife," said President Barack Obama, author of such best-selling books as "The Audacity of Hope: Thoughts on reclaiming the American dream," and "Dreams From my Father: A story of race and inheritance."

Yes, amid today's ferocious and unforgiving media frenzy, at least in some regards an individual lacks any bragging rights to "celebrity" status without having at least one self-written book.

Books Help Put Everyday People "On the Map"

Following the lead put in place by growing numbers of politicians and celebrities, virtually every "big name" in the media has rushed to put his or her book onto the market as fast and as efficiently as possible.

Besides celebrities who earned their fame in the entertainment world, just about every major sitting politician and popular budding candidates for elected office has released a book chronicling his or her life or philosophies.

Political conservatives and national office candidates Sarah Palin and Newt Gingrich have been among big-name personalities who stampeded into the book market as fast as they could possibly manage. Numerous and complex strategies come to play as these political combatants, big-name celebrities and "everyday people" rush their publications to market.

Yes, amid today's ferocious and unforgiving media frenzy, at least in some regards an individual lacks any bragging rights to "celebrity" status without having at least one self-written book.

And, any "expert," analyst or politician seemingly risks being labeled as frivolous or unsubstantial if lacking a substantive publication to at least promote or mention.

"Literature adds to reality, it does not simply describe it," said Clive Staples "C.S." Lewis, a 20th Century British academic, novelist and literary critic. "It enriches the necessary competencies that everyday life requires and provides; and, in this respect, it irrigates the deserts that our lives have already become."

Take Advantage of the Public's Needs

Today's celebrity-obsessed society deeply craves knowledge, entertainment and vital information to help put people onto a path for wealth, success or survival.

Those of us who realize and target these vital factors are able to seize and satisfy apparent public demand. Whether we embrace or despise President Obama's political philosophies, for instance, there can be little denying that his initial books generated the bulk of his personal fortune.

Although an increasingly successful social services volunteer whose political career catapulted into his mid-40s, it wasn't until this Harvard Law School graduate published books that he became a multi-millionaire many times over.

Like the late President John F. Kennedy, who wrote the Pulitzer Prize-winning "Profiles in Courage" in 1955, Obama sought and received

Whether we embrace or despise President Obama's political philosophies, for instance, there can be little denying that his initial books generated the bulk of his personal fortune.

assistance and financial rewards from a standard, mainstream and well-established publishing company.

Although numerous mainstream book publishers sign lucrative contracts with lots of today's primary celebrities, TV personalities and radio commentators, streams of budding or increasingly popular individuals are latching onto other publication methods.

Improved Technologies Give the "Little Guy" a Shot

A vastly growing number of fine-tuned publishing systems have steadily enabled the so-called "regular person" and even current big-name personalities to get their books published and made available to the whole world—at little or no production cost.

This marks a sharp contrast to the pre-21st Century era. Until around 2005-2008, streams of optimistic and hopeful book writers had to depend on limited numbers of mainstream publishers to give the "green light" on production proposals.

At the time, for the most part self-publishing seemed a risky, arduous and even foolish option. Many who chose this route got stuck with many hundreds or thousands of books collecting dust in their garages or rented storage units.

A huge majority of aspiring writers got a maze of

rejection form-letters. Frustrated and discouraged potential authors often found these unwanted notices stuffed into their old-style snail-mail boxes by the dozens or even hundreds.

Sadly, until the latest technological developments of the past several years, the mainstream, standard publishing companies held virtually all of the proverbial playing cards in the book world.

This pernicious, cruel and sometimes greedy system sometimes left super-talented and aspiring writers at the mercy of greedy publishing companies—many based in New York City. Often left with little bargaining power, some authors lucky enough to land contracts got miniscule royalty percentages or shamelessly low advances. Some of the world's most popular authors endured such hardship before achieving fame. Among them:

Harper Lee: According to various media accounts, this Pulitzer Prize-winning author received at least 30 rejection letters from publishers before finally landing a contract for her classic 1960 novel "To Kill a Mockingbird." The basis for an Academy Award®-award winning film by the same name starring Gregory Peck, the book is considered by many literary critics as among the greatest all-time American classics.

JK Rowling: Born Joanne "Jo" Rowling in England in the summer of 1965, she was a 30-year-old, divorced mother of one child in 1996 upon finishing her first book manuscript, "Harry

Dozens of mainstream publishing companies rejected Rowling's initial book proposals until a small London-based publishing company, Bloomsbury, purchased rights to print an initial 1,000 copies.

Potter and the Philosopher's Stone." Dozens of mainstream publishing companies rejected Rowling's initial book proposals until a small London-based publishing company, Bloomsbury, purchased rights to print an initial 1,000 copies. The book's popularity skyrocketed, sparking the "Harry Potter" book series that eventually earned Rowling a fortune reportedly exceeding well over $1 billion.

Charles Dickens: The 19th century author of numerous classics, this native of Portsmouth, Hampshire, in England, desperately needed money for the necessary medical care during the pregnancy of his wife Catherine Thomson Hogarth in 1843. Determined to generate personal funds, Dickens wrote the classic "A Christmas Carol" featuring Ebenezer Scrooge and spent his own money to publish the book. A publisher had initially offered Dickens a lump sum for the manuscript, but instead the author chose to fund the book's publication himself in hopes that a percentage of the profits would result in more income. Dickens finished writing "A Christmas Carol" in early December, the book was printed on the 17th of that month, and by Christmas Eve eager buyers snatched up all 6,000 copies from the initial printing.

Today's Technology Gives You the Key to Potential Success

Success stories such as those enjoyed by Rowling, Lee and Dickens often hinge largely upon an author's own dogged determination when dealing with mainstream publishers.

But think of the many potential classics through the past several generations that readers have never enjoyed. Sadly, no one will ever know the precise number of writers of the likes of Rowling and Lee who never got their books published.

On the positive side, however, steadily growing numbers of today's authors are using low-cost technologies to get their books self-published—in some cases clearing the way for run-away Number-One national best-sellers. Among these success stories:

Kathryn Stockett: Born in Jackson, Mississippi, in 1969, she was reared for the most part by an African-American maid during her mother's frequent absences. A veteran of the New York City publishing industry, Stockett pulled her personal early-life experiences as the basis for her best-selling novel, "The Help." But according to "USA Today," Stockett received at least 60 rejections from publishers. Undaunted, Stockett persisted in her pitch efforts, until the book was finally published in 2009. By August 2011, "The Help" had spent more than 100 weeks on the "New York Times Best Seller" list, generating at least 5 million sales. The basis for a hit movie by the same

25

> Rather than face consistent rejection from mainstream publishers, Burpo contracted with a Tennessee-based publisher of Christian books and Bibles, Thomas Nelson.

name, the book is published by Berkley Trade Publishers, a division of the Penguin Group. The book also inspired a hit movie by the same name.

Todd Burpo: His book, "Heaven is for Real: A little boy's astounding story of his trip to heaven and back," skyrocketed into best-seller status over a multi-month period in 2011. With the help of writer Lynn Vincent, Burpo, a pastor in Imperial, Nebraska, wrote this compelling 192-page book to chronicle the real-life story of his son. At age 4, Colton slipped from consciousness during surgery, before telling relatives what they considered riveting and irrefutable stories of a visit to Jesus in heaven. Rather than face consistent rejection from mainstream publishers, Burpo contracted with a Tennessee-based publisher of Christian books and Bibles, Thomas Nelson.

We expect that like Burpo and Stockett, steadily growing numbers of authors nationwide will either seek the assistance of smaller book publishing houses or proceed directly to low-cost self-publishing methods now available to the masses—not just wealthy celebrities.

Success Stories Abound

Countless self-published books have catapulted into best-seller status, turning their writers into instant legends in the literary world. Such resounding grand slams should pick up pace during the next few years, thanks to easy-to-implement on-demand printing services available to almost anyone.

Just some of the many champions have included John Grisham, who self-published his first novel, "A Time to Kill," in 1989. Grisham initially sold those early books from his car trunk before emerging as among the world's most popular authors of legal thrillers.

Frustrated with the big corporate publishing houses, H. Jackson Brown self-published his "Life's Little Instruction Book," which went on to sell 5 million copies while soaring to the top of the New York Times Bestseller List.

Just as impressive, author Aliske Webb got 150 rejection letters from greedy mainstream publishers. Webb self-published "Twelve Golden Threads," which sold 25,000 copies before the giant HarperCollins signed her to a four-book contract.

The numerous other mega-success stories of self-published books include: "Dianetics," by L. Ron Hubbard, 20 million copies; "In Search of Excellence," by Tom Peters, initially 25,000 copies under self-publication before selling 10 million copies via Warner; and "The Joy of Cooking" by Irma Rombauer, initially self-published in 1931 before being picked up by Scribners, which now sells 100,000 copies yearly.

"While no one can ever guarantee success in self-publishing, anyone who has a unique story

New just-in-time, low-cost and efficient publishing operations has opened the door to many people who once saw their opportunities closed early on.

or a marvelous how-to idea would be foolish to pass up today's inexpensive self-publishing opportunities," Wayne says. "Since the process is relatively easy, the time to act is now rather than later."

Chapter
3

Famous and Little-Known
People Seek Value

Thanks largely to the advent of new publishing technology, we're ready, willing and able to assist qualified celebrities and even little-known folks from throughout America. We help position clients for the possibility of achieving their dreams in the publishing world.

Because we work behind the scenes, we're unable to publicly identify the growing number of individuals who have sought our assistance. Naturally, as you might very well imagine, many of these individuals express their gratitude when we help make their dreams come true.

Some of our greatest joy comes from the ability to consider the many authors as perhaps the latest literary successes, such as the JK Rowlings and Harper Lees of the world who have been cruelly rejected by humongous, big-money publishing companies.

Besides getting much-deserved recognition, getting your own book published and onto the market generates seemingly endless potential benefits.

New just-in-time, low-cost and efficient publishing operations has opened the door to many people who once saw their opportunities closed early on. To some, this transition sparkles as if the gates to heaven have swung wide open.

"We must accept finite disappointment, but never lose infinite hope," said the Rev. Dr. Martin Luther King Jr., the civil rights icon of the mid-20th Century.

Discover the Many Positive Possibilities of Book Publishing

Besides getting much-deserved recognition, getting your own book published and onto the market generates seemingly endless potential benefits.

While too numerous to list in full, these positive possibilities can position even a novice for great new opportunities. Among just some of the many attributes:

Income potential: Although no one should ever guarantee that you'll sell even a single book, the possibility of generating a moderate or substantial income comes to play. Authors position themselves for a chance to earn thousands or even millions of dollars.

Recognition: Merely being able to show someone a book featuring your byline immediately puts you into a new and higher league. Many first-time authors recall that upon initial publication, their many friends started seeing them in an all-new light.

Legitimacy: Many first-time authors get instant recognition as experts, especially if their publications deal with specific "how-to" topics, scientific theories, political analysis or the scientific realm.

Exposure: Because they're now viewed as experts thanks to their books, authors seize the possibility of getting invitations onto TV shows, radio programs, educational sessions or even "how-to" seminars where participants pay to see presentations.

Increased demand: Some first-time authors who were once shunned by their peers or ignored by various media outlets suddenly discover that they're now deluged with appearance offers.

"I have personally experienced at least some of these benefits first-hand, almost right away," some first-time authors might say. "If I had known that such a project would have put me onto such a higher playing field, believe me I would have done this much sooner."

All along, remember that age-old saying, "success breeds success." Many first-time authors find right away that writing, creating and publishing a book can become addicting and difficult to stop.

For most, this evolves into far more than a mere

"How much will all this cost, and how can I get my books published and marketed?"

"ego trip," but rather a genuine attempt to help other people and to fulfill their educational, emotional, spiritual, or health needs.

Discover Where to Start in Your Book Publishing Journey

For many people initially delving into the possibility of getting their first book published, marketed and distributed, just starting such a process might seem daunting and perhaps even a bit overwhelming.

"How should I start?" You might ask yourself at the very beginning. "What are the right things for me to do? What steps should I take to achieve such success? How much will all this cost, and how can I get my books published and marketed?"

While all these important and essential questions emerge as a natural and essential part of the process, many potential first-time authors admit to themselves right away: "I don't know how to write at all. I'm incapable of expressing myself in a compelling, logical and understandable way."

Meantime, as if all these many concerns weren't already enough to worry about, another essential challenge also rises: "I'm busy every moment of the day, and I haven't got time to spare. How in the world could I ever get enough time?"

Well, this is where experts such as us come

into the picture. As seasoned professionals in writing, book publishing, image development and marketing, we're among the world's seasoned and highly experienced advisors and consultants positioned to assist and help lead new authors onto a path to potential success.

"Every student deserves to be treated as a potential genius," said Anton Ehrenzweig, an early- and mid-20th Century German native who immigrated to England. He played an integral role in discovering how the unconscious mind generates creativity, analysis and dynamic mental processes—such as in the development and creation of artwork.

Right from the start, anyone considering or planning an initial book should get at least a brief, basic understanding of today's intricate publishing world.

Understand the Basics of the Book Publishing Business

Right from the start, anyone considering or planning an initial book should get at least a brief, basic understanding of today's intricate publishing world.

To be quite honest, in essence the book publishing and marketing industry finds itself locked in the midst of tremendous, persistent industry-wide chaos.

For the most part much-needed technological changes have essentially turned the whole industry upside down.

More than ever before, the entire market has

Emerging high-quality, and easy-to-use self-publishing systems have flooded the market with new first-time authors, giving consumers more options than ever.

begun to spin into a non-stop state of influx, to the point where even seasoned long-time professionals lack any full understanding of where the industry is headed. Anyone who claims otherwise is trying to feed you a line of bull.

Three primary factors have kicked this transition into full gear:

Competition: New cost-efficient, quick-to-start and real-time publishing systems have knocked some big corporate publishing houses off their undeserved pedestals.

New sector: The steadily increasing popularity of digital eBooks rather than just standard "dead-tree" printed books has shot deep into the overall market.

Product fluctuations: Emerging high-quality, and easy-to-use self-publishing systems have flooded the market with new first-time authors, giving consumers more options than ever.

Partly as a result of varying degrees of these factors, the standard longtime printing and brick-and-mortar book stores have felt a strong impact.

We equate this to the widespread slump in the U.S. Postal service, once considered a milestone system that for a time had been projected to remain strong, vibrant and robust for many hundreds of years to come.

But during the first decade of this century, the

Post Office suffered major multi-billion-dollar budget shortfalls when most consumers started receiving and paying their regular monthly bills online.

Well, similar developments in digital technology also have walloped the bookstore industry. In the summer of 2011, this pernicious whirlpool forced Borders Book Stores nationwide to announce the closure of hundreds of its brick-and-mortar outlets.

Sales of eBooks Skyrocketed Worldwide

Analysts cited a surge in demand for eBooks, so large and steady that the giant online Amazon.com book sales service announced that for the first time more than half of its sales were in electronic form.

Increasingly large percentages of eBook buyers prefer to read such presentations on Kindle™ devices, proudly described by Amazon—the primary distributor of such units—as "The #1 Bestselling eReader in the World."

Word of this monumental book industry transition kicked into full gear as book publishers, agents and distributors gathered in New York City in the summer of 2011 for their annual seminar. As reported by the "New York Times" and other media outlets, many seasoned industry professionals at the gathering admitted that few of their colleagues—if any—seemed to know

As reported by the "New York Times" and other media outlets, many seasoned industry professionals at the gathering admitted that few of their colleagues—if any—seemed to know precisely where their industry was heading.

precisely where their industry was heading.

Among those that the media described as admittedly perplexed was Golden Globe®-award winning actor John Lithgow, who reportedly planned to release his own book as that summer waned. Ironically, during the same period Lithgow was scheduled to appear in the title role in a Broadway production of "The Columnist," portraying the famously meticulous newspaper writer Joseph Alsop.

"All the best stories in the world are but one story in reality—the story of escape," said Walter Bagehot, a 19th Century English journalist, essayist and businessman. "It is the only thing which interests us all, and at all times how to escape."

This strikes us as an intriguing and paradoxical commentary, at least when considered in terms of today's slippery and unpredictable book business.

"Trends in the book industry point to a need for increased efficiency and flexibility," an industry official told Publishers Weekly amid the height of this transition. "We are working with printing and publishing firms to share rapidly evolving opportunities and challenges facing the industries today. With these shared insights, we can work together to accommodate adoption in areas with highest returns and develop better solutions year after year."

Such self-serving analysis and blatant linguistic hogwash reveals to us that the industry has a serious "weak spot" that aspiring authors can benefit from if they seize such opportunity in a quick, timely manner.

All Book Sales Surged Despite the Weak International Economy

Despite persistent and unpredictable chaos within the entire book industry, the "New York Times" reported that overall sales of "dead-tree books" and eBooks increased—even amid the international economic slump.

"We're seeing a resurgence, and we're seeing it across all markets—trade, academic and professional," Tina Jordan, the vice president of the Association of American Publishers told the newspaper. "In each category we're seeing growth. The printed word is alive and well whether it takes a paper delivery or a digital delivery."

To back up this claim, Jordan noted that the sales of higher-education books were especially strong, selling $4.55 billion in 2010, up 18.7 percent since 2007, the "New York Times" said.

Other primary and essential market segments also enjoyed overall sales boots, including for various trade industries, juvenile books, the young-adult segment and dystopian fiction. With a three-year increase at 8.8 percent, the adult fiction market enjoyed a sizable increase as well.

"The printed word is alive and well whether it takes a paper delivery or a digital delivery."
-Tina Jordan

Yet what does this increase in demand mean for our clients?

"While there are never any guarantees, this surge in demand can evolve into great potential for new or even seasoned authors," we tell any current or potential client who might ask. "The time has never been better to latch on to such opportunity."

Chapter
4

Position Yourself for Potential Literary Success

Fully aware and cognizant of the many flaws now permeating the book industry, we're among analysts, experts and publishers who view this as an excellent time for seasoned or even first-time authors to jump into the fray.

The key here is to realize that streams of celebrities, hosts and analysts all continue to publish their own books or to seek lucrative contracts with established publishers for a vital reason. Namely, despite the intense instability in the overall market, huge money-making opportunities exist in the field—perhaps to a greater degree than ever.

Just as important, the low-cost, quick-time publishing systems also enable regular, everyday, little-known writers and citizens to enter this potentially lucrative arena.

The key here is to seize the moment. Get into the

Just as important, the low-cost, quick-time publishing systems also enable regular, everyday, little-known writers and citizens to enter this potentially lucrative arena.

action now while the fire heats up, and like many new authors you could very well position yourself for possible success. As some analysts have concluded, "there's no time better than the present to enter the game."

The Nike™ shoe-production company has long been acclaimed in part for its world-famous tagline, "Just do it." Seasoned and novice athletes, business leaders, entrepreneurs and artists often instinctively realize that victory only becomes possible by first entering the playing field.

John Edward "Jack" Walsh Jr., former president of General Electric, has been quoted as saying that "giving people self-confidence is by far the most important thing that I can do, because then they will act."

Benefit From a Seasoned Expert or Coach

Just like a professional athlete, an aspiring first-time movie actor, or a novice taking ballroom dance lessons for the first time, when launching your book career be sure to seek the continual guidance or advice of a seasoned expert in this arena.

Remain careful to check for and require that your mentor possess expertise in graphic design, image development, publishing, pricing, product placement, marketing and personal communication skills such as public speaking.

Meantime, some first-time authors decide early in the process to avoid attempts at publicity or widespread sales. For the most part the bulk of people within this class strive mainly to leave an enduring legacy for their children, grandchildren and subsequent generations. These strategies are far more than merely admirable; they're commendable.

The term "carpe diem," meaning "seize the day," from a classic work by Horace in the century immediately before Christ's birth, fits marvelously in this regard. As corny as such a statement might sound, each of us has only one life to live. Without grasping vital opportunities when they arise, we fail to grow intellectually, spiritually and financially.

"Nothing builds self-esteem and self-confidence like accomplishment," said Thomas Carlyle, a 19th Century Victorian-era Scottish satirist, historian, essayist and teacher.

Death Robs Us of Those Who Fail to Chronicle their Lives

Far more times than we would like to remember, on occasion our efforts have focused on fruitless attempts to encourage extremely mature people in their 80s or 90s to chronicle their life stories.

The standard four-paragraph death notice system fails to come even close to describing the rich, full and compelling lives of these departed souls.

Sadly, in some of these instances, although these individuals were vibrant and in good health at the time, they or their relatives failed to seize the opportunity before death or illness won out. So, now the personal stories and wisdoms of these now-departed people are lost to the world forever.

Will you allow such an ending to befall you or your relatives, when knowing full well that an affordable, relatively easy and satisfying solution exists?

Our hearts sink when obituaries hit the newspapers briefly giving public notice that people have died, those whom we had encouraged—but failed to convince—to chronicle their lives. The standard four-paragraph death notice system fails to come even close to describing the rich, full and compelling lives of these departed souls. Their many accomplishments, joys, sorrows and transitions become lost from history forever.

"I have never killed a man, but I have read many obituaries with great pleasure," said Clarence Darrow, a sophisticated country American lawyer in the late 1800s and early 1900s, known for his wit, agnosticism and willingness to fight for civil liberties.

Ultimately, the choice rests with you, on whether to seize today's low-cost opportunities to bring your life, thoughts, philosophies or creative stories to the world. Once making that stupendous decision, your unique book can get on track within mere weeks or months.

Aim Your Cross-Hairs on a Target Market

The first, primary and essential step before writing a book always involves focusing on the need to identify your target market. These individuals, groups or organizations hold the distinction of serving as the most likely individuals to purchase what you hope to offer.

For instance, at least most of the time, a how-to book detailing the intricacies, skills and "tricks" used in fly fishing serve a much different specific audience than the potential buyers of health books—although some market overlapping can occur.

Consider for instance the case of one of our most cherished friends, a 65-year-old fly-fishing enthusiast. We noticed several books about this activity in his house before the man suffered severe back problems that prevented him from engaging in his cherished pastime. Concerned, we gave him one of our ghost-written books about pain.

"To the winner goes the spoils," an age-old saying promises. Even more compelling, those of us who realize the vital need to find and fulfill the needs

"To the winner goes the spoils," an age-old saying promises. Even more compelling, those of us who realize the vital need to find and fulfill the needs of a vibrant target market can position ourselves for tremendous success.

For most people, anywhere from four hours to a full day of diverse, concise and highly focused research can glean the basics necessary to launch a book project.

of a vibrant target market can position ourselves for tremendous success.

"Advertising people who ignore research are as dangerous as generals who ignore decades of enemy signals," said David Ogilvy, the late, widely acclaimed British marketing executive often hailed as "the father of advertising."

Careful to follow such essential strategies, both seasoned and novice writers who want success must grab and amass as much information as they can about consumers likely to want their books.

Where do these potential buyers live? With just as much urgency, a lengthy list of other potential vital factors include everything from gender, income, and education, to how these individuals might benefit from the story, tips or teachings that you can provide.

Conduct Essential, Quick, Fast & Accurate Research

Today's Internet provides instant, voluminous and often-accurate information. Savvy, quickly compiled research can pinpoint everything from demographic data, published sales totals for specific types of items, and even trends on public opinions and changing preferences.

For most people, anywhere from four hours to a full day of diverse, concise and highly focused research can glean the basics necessary to launch a book project. Once these findings come to play, an ideal time arises to ask vital questions necessary to make success possible.

Besides determining consumer preferences and a buyer's average budget, the most helpful data also should chronicle at least a generalized summary of books, periodicals or TV shows that already cover your preferred or chosen topic.

A strong and fairly reliable tool for tackling this essential phase usually involves a visit to the world's largest and most comprehensive online book sales site, Amazon.com. Browse the website to determine the primary books already offered within your chosen or preferred sector.

Amid this research, consider such questions as: Is my potential target market already served? What new, interesting, educational or controversial information can I introduce to this sector?

For at least the past several generations, many sales experts and literary professionals have insisted essentially that: "There are only 34 different types of story plots, and virtually all of them have been told in some form or other. Only the names, places and eras of the characters change."

"There are only 34 different types of story plots, and virtually all of them have been told in some form or other. Only the names, places and eras of the characters change."

Although brick-and-mortar book stores such as Borders closed amid an overall upheaval and massive industry-wide change, consumers still yearn for information and for stories that they deem essential to their happiness or even for their survival

Some observers also tell us that the same holds true for nonfiction books or how-to publications. Indeed, much of the time current publications and the endless power of the Web already get covered in full-blown, extensive detail.

Yet, if these assumptions are indeed true, why are sales of paper books or "dead-tree" publications, and eBooks continuing to surge? As the first decade of the 21st Century ended, well past the advent of the Internet, the Book Industry Study Group reported that publishers' net revenues had risen 1 percent year-to-year to an annual $43.2 billion.

Once again here, we feel the need to stress the fact that demand for fiction and non-fiction books continued to swell, despite the debilitating international economic slump. Although brick-and-mortar book stores such as Borders closed amid an overall upheaval and massive industry-wide change, consumers still yearn for information and for stories that they deem essential to their happiness or even for their survival or potential prosperity.

Appreciate Two Critical Words

As an experienced or a new book-writer, you can position yourself to benefit by keeping two vital words at the forefront of your projects—"knowledge" and "power."

Essentially, the public desperately craves simple, concise and accurate information. The phrase made famous 400 years ago by English philosopher Sir Francis Bacon, "Knowledge is power" holds true now perhaps more than ever before.

Determined to survive amid economic calamity or to better themselves through educational materials, consumers are often willing and eager to pay substantial amounts to get what they consider: "Essential information that I can benefit from right away."

Among perhaps the world's best experts at offering the public unique and critical information that investors yearn to receive, our good friend William F. "Bill" McCready developed the popular and extremely helpful "Futures Trading Secrets™" website and publication.

McCready helps satisfy and meet the public's yearning for valuable and helpful information on how to successfully trade via the Internet on the futures market. A genius and a whiz with numbers and charts, McCready created a unique, compelling system only accessible via his Website and book.

Like McCready and countless other highly successful authors have, you can find a niche and offer that market unique information it desperately craves—data found nowhere else on the Internet or within books already in print.

Among our steadily growing cadre of books worth noting in this regard, all available for purchase at Amazon.com or through special orders from any major bookstore.

Determined to survive amid economic calamity or to better themselves through educational materials, consumers are often willing and eager to pay substantial amounts to get what they consider: "Essential

We Find and Target Markets for Ourselves and for Clients

Determined to practice what we preach, we—the authors of this book—discovered formerly underserved market niches. After compiling and analyzing consumer information, working as a team, we wrote, designed and published several books produced to give consumers information and skills they need to thrive in a tough economy.

Among our steadily growing cadre of books worth noting in this regard, all available for purchase at Amazon.com or through special orders from any major bookstore:

Ask: Play the Asking Game and Take the Path to What You Want: Authored by Wayne Rollan Melton, and featuring a foreword by Patty Melton, this 187-page book is printed through our Fix Bay Inc Publishing division. Readers learn the vital essentials on how to ask for what they want in life, plus helpful negotiation techniques designed to help increase the probability of getting what they want. Our research indicates that these specific strategies developed and fine-tuned by Wayne are found nowhere else in any other book or on the Internet.

How to Eliminate Fear of Global Economic Recession and Terrorism: Written by Wayne, and featuring an overall design and image created by Patty, this 173-page book, also offered via our Fix Bay Inc Publishing company, features Wayne's compilation of a unique, never-told-before accumulation of systems that people can use to survive and thrive during persistent recession and nagging terrorism. Once again, through a melding of information sources and our own image development, this book was designed to satisfy the public's never-ending hunger for vital and useful information.

As demand for our services increased during the past decade, we have continually helped our steadily growing list of clients write, create and publish books on a vast array of topics. These ranged from a health book on how to remain youthful, featuring a foreword by a Number One-selling author, to critical advice from an alcoholic who robbed dozens of grocery stores. In essence, all these projects were spun and designed in a manner hailed as a unique opportunity for consumers to benefit from critical information.

As demand for our services increased during the past decade, we have continually helped our steadily growing list of clients write, create and publish books on a vast array of topics.

Chapter
5

Take a Vital Leadership Role

Whether writing about your life experiences or giving "how-to" information, you can and should assume a powerful leadership role in conveying your message.

This way, you'll generate a unique and potentially valuable spin into your book. When chronicling your life, tell the reader how to benefit from—or how to learn lessons about—personal successes and failures that you experienced.

With just as much vibrancy and passion, give your "how-to" books or historical chronicles a forceful, spicy flavor laced with your strong and passionate opinions on critical issues.

With just as much fervor, give your own critical and sharp analysis of the facts on controversial problems. Potential topics might range from the morality of drag-racing through residential neighborhoods to whether the media used correct info on a hot issue.

"Always be yourself, express yourself, have faith in yourself," said Bruce Lee, a Chinese American movie actor, philosopher and martial arts champion who died in 1973 at age 32. ""Do not go out and look for a successful personality and duplicate it."

Sure enough, as Herbert Marshall McLuhan, a Canadian philosopher, author and scholar, stated so eloquently and succinctly before his death in 1980: "The medium is the message." Some analysts have even concluded that McLuhan even predicted the Internet more than 30 years before the Web entered the mainstream worldwide culture.

"The medium is the message." Some analysts have even concluded that McLuhan even predicted the Internet more than 30 years before the Web entered the mainstream worldwide culture.

In essence, McLuhan proclaimed that the medium in which we use to convey a message influences how the public perceives that specific communication.

While embracing this theory and taking McLuhan's suggestions to heart, we agree with marketing analysts who insist that "having a controversial or unique dead-tree book to promote can give a 'regular guy' or a celebrity far more credibility than simply posting on a blog, throwing a greasy low-budget video up on YouTube.com or writing a letter to the editor of your local newspaper." Yes, having a cutting-edge book can and will give you instant credibility and legitimacy in the public mindset.

"I'm finding that I can accomplish this," many clients invariably tell us. "I had no idea beforehand this process would be so educational. I've discovered new details about my topic that I didn't even know before.

Enjoy Your Book Like a Fish Takes to Water

A handful of first-time authors start behaving in a timid manner during the initial research and writing phase. Invariably a vast majority of these people soon leave such anxious behavior behind and instead quickly find great joy in the process.

Especially when working with seasoned writing experts and image advisors such as us, a vast majority of budding authors make many unexpected discoveries.

"I'm finding that I can accomplish this," many clients invariably tell us. "I had no idea beforehand this process would be so educational. I've discovered new details about my topic that I didn't even know before. Even better than that, another unexpected surprise emerged. I enjoy this work far more than I thought before. Now, I'm addicted to getting as many high-quality, useful books on the market as I possibly can."

In all honesty, some of our clients find themselves becoming "too passionate" about a particular project. Many of these evolving authors enjoy the creation phase so much that they essentially "never realize when to put the project to bed."

To put this into clear perspective, envision a professional, highly acclaimed watercolor portrait artist. After working countless hours for many days, weeks or months on a single portrait, the artist might at some point initially consider the work as complete.

At that particular juncture, any effort to continue adding layers of unnecessary color would essentially only "muddy the waters." When adding far more color than necessary, the result sometimes evolves into a cloudy, dirtied and difficult-to-decipher image—all because the artist refused to acknowledge and to appreciate the proper time to stop.

Well, the same danger holds true for first-time writers and even some widely acclaimed, seasoned professional authors as well. Seasoned marketers and advisors can play a pivotal role in determining where a particular project might need more work, or to identify high-quality sections of a manuscript that lack any need for fine-tuning.

Always Remember: "Write to Sell"

Jump into your book development and creation process with a write-to-sell attitude. Every step of the way you should remain focused in delivering prose in a compelling, informational and concise manner. To accomplish this:

Compelling: With each new turn and twist, always leave a crisp, energetic and increasingly tense sense that "there is more vital information to follow."

> Jump into your book development and creation process with a write-to-sell attitude.

Surprise: From page-to-page, load the manuscript with surprises, while careful to avoid taking a predictable route.

Passion: With slowly increasing intensity, display a steadily increasing sense of passion. Think of a rose opening at sunrise, always revealing more beauty with each new second.

Love: Write in a way that shows readers your genuine "love" for them, conveying a message that you genuinely care for them and want them to succeed.

Self-appreciation: Ultimately, you should write the kind of book that you would want to read yourself. So, avoid attempts to "try to be something that you're not."

Unique: Strive to set your own trend, positioning yourself as a "leader." To do this, show courage while unafraid to take a strong, vibrant opinion on difficult issues.

Accuracy: At all times, strive to convey accurate, cohesive information. Otherwise, you will lose all credibility, hurting chances people will want to buy your book.

John Jakes, an American writer best known for his historical fiction, has been quoted as saying: "Be yourself. Above all, let who you are, what you are, what you believe, shine through every sentence you write, every piece you finish."

Consider Using an Experienced, Highly Successful Ghostwriter

"Write to be understood, speak to be heard, (and) read to grow," said Lawrence Clark Powell, a 20th Century literary critic and author of more than 100 books.

For the vast majority of people, however— everyone from celebrities to everyday citizens— the mere notion of writing an entire book can emerge as a mighty tall order.

Herein rests a primary reason why even the most successful fiction and non-fiction authors today often employ the services of ghostwriters. The term "ghost" comes to play, because the names of these professionals never get credited.

Essentially, an effective, seasoned and highly creative ghostwriter works as a "hired gun," someone paid to work in the background to position a project for potential success.

The most seasoned, successful and highly successful ghostwriters can often crank out high-quality, readable, magnetic book manuscripts within a matter of several months.

By contrast, a book-writing novice or rookie might take several years to complete an initial draft, a slop of literary hogwash deemed unsuitable for publication.

Yet we suspect that a vast majority of the most successful books, particularly those marketed as written by celebrities, were actually crafted by ghostwriters.

"The only difficulty of literature is not to write, but to write what you mean," said Robert Lewis Stevenson, the 19th Century author of such classics as "Kidnapped," "Treasure Island," and "The Strange Case of Dr. Jekyll and Mr. Hyde."

Skilled Ghostwriters Let You Take the Glory

A highly skilled, seasoned and fine-tuned ghostwriter enables you to "take all the glory." The listed author who hired the ghostwriter steps into the public limelight, while the "hired gun" who did the bulk of the actual work hides in a proverbial back seat.

Eager to benefit from such professionals, huge percentages of celebrities and "everyday folks" with best-selling books have employed ghostwriters.

Large publishing houses and printers serving authors who produce their own books seem to lack specific statistics on precisely how many books are ghost-written. Yet we suspect that a vast majority of the most successful books, particularly those marketed as written by celebrities, were actually crafted by ghostwriters.

But where do you find a ghostwriter? How much do such services cost? How long will the writing process take?

Ultimately, in today's fast-paced, high-tech world the answers to these questions are paradoxical—both easy and complex at the same time. This is certainly far from a one-answer-fits-all situation, since lots of vital and intermixed variables come to play.

Much of the time, people also comment that they have always wanted to write their own books, or that they once met an author.

You Have Probably Never Met a Successful Book Ghostwriter

At least based on what we've seen, read and heard, the vast majority of people in the United States have never met a full-time, highly successful book ghostwriter.

"I love seeing the reactions people have, when we're at parties and people meet Wayne for the first time," Patty sometimes says to her many friends. "Most of the time, the first reaction many people have when they learn that Wayne is a ghostwriter is, "Wow! That's interesting. I've never met someone who does that before. You mean, there really are ghostwriters—they really exist?'"

We each can testify from personal experience that from this point forward, many people then throw out corny jokes about "ghosts." Much of the time, people also comment that they have always wanted to write their own books, or that they once met an author.

Still, despite these pleasant but brief interludes

From what we can tell, the vast majority of successful book ghostwriters live near the highest concentrations of big-corporate publishing houses—primarily in the New York City and Los Angeles areas.

and introductions, many people leave perplexed about the entire ghostwriting and book-publishing process.

The mere notion seems to strike many average citizens as if science fiction. Mesmerized, a majority of these individuals seem to believe they have as much chance at getting a book published as having a flying saucer land in their front yards.

"It's kind of fun to do the impossible," said Walt Disney, the late creator of the world-famous Disneyland amusement park and producer of hundreds of hit family movies.

Snatch Up an Experienced Ghostwriter Fast

The U.S. Census Bureau has never published statistics on the number of full-time ghostwriters—particularly those professionals who specialize in books.

At least judging by word-of-mouth information, huge swaths of entire states apparently have only a handful of seasoned, successful book ghostwriters or none at all. From what we can tell, the vast majority of successful book ghostwriters live near the highest concentrations of big-corporate publishing houses—primarily in the New York City and Los Angeles areas.

Compounding the problem from the standpoint

of hopeful authors, the literary community fails to maintain a single, comprehensive listing of such professionals. Nonetheless, there are some solutions for those willing to hunt for such pros. Among them:

Big publishing houses: Before beginning to write, some celebrities and "everyday people" contact several of the major mainstream book publishing companies such as Random House, Penguin Books, or many others. Yet merely asking for references will not necessarily result in an answer. So, intense or in-depth "print-my-idea" pitches might become necessary just to get a referral. Even worse, some publishers might require reaching a book contract with them first, and the odds of that happening are astronomical unless you happen to be "a household name."

Literary agent: Prior to any attempts to write, some aspiring authors strive to form an alliance or contract with a seasoned or well-connected literary agent. To vastly increase the odds of this happening, you likely would need a "killer" idea or concept, or happen to shine in the public mindset as a celebrity.

Writer services: Hundreds of aspiring writers pitch their services online at Websites such as eLance, desperate for work in today's harsh economy. Many writers bid their services at the lowest possible price, sometimes below minimum wage. But the "buyer should beware," since huge

To vastly increase the odds of this happening, you likely would need a "killer" idea or concept, or happen to shine in the public mindset as a celebrity.

Possessing a comprehensive knowledge of what you can and cannot say in an article or book can go a long way in preventing a multi-million-dollar civil judgment against you.

percentages of these so-called "experienced" writers live in third-world countries or nations such as India and China—and their English skills are extremely limited.

Hiring questionable or fly-by-night writers for rock-bottom pay poses serious dangers, opening up a Pandora's Box of potential lawsuits for anyone foolish enough to hire them.

Sadly, many celebrities and "everyday people" would not know what "good, fantastic writing is, even if it slapped them in the face." As a result, a sloppy, untrained or poorly educated writer could submit a proverbial "pile of hogwash as a manuscript, and the unsuspected and untrained buyer would not know any better."

Worsening matters, writers from third-world countries and even rookie authors fresh out of the U.S. collegial system lack a necessary full understanding of American libel law. Possessing a comprehensive knowledge of what you can and cannot say in an article or book can go a long way in preventing a multi-million-dollar civil judgment against you.

Just one unintended slip-up could mean the loss of big bucks from your personal checking account.

Follow these Critical Suggestions

Fully cognizant of the numerous proverbial land minds surrounding the literary playing field, we strongly suggest following these basic, easy-to-understand criteria:

Experience: Seek the guidance and help of a ghostwriter who has worked in the industry full-time for at least a full decade.

History: Only consider the services of an author who has written at least 25 books, and preferably much more than that.

Success: The writer should be able to give you success stories, such as working for clients who have reached the top of the New York Times Bestseller List.

Education: Our experience shows that the best, most compelling and fruitful ghost-writing efforts are created by individuals who have earned college degrees in literature or journalism.

Past jobs: Before becoming a full-time ghostwriter, the person should have worked as a reporter, columnist or editor for a respected newspaper, magazine or publishing house.

At this juncture, we feel a need to point out—in a "shameless self-promotion"—that Wayne fits the bill here in every regard. A former Editor-on-Loan to "USA Today," the nation's largest newspaper, Wayne has written dozens of books. Some of his projects have been for high-profile clients, including indirectly for a celebrity who reached the Number One position on the New York Times Best-seller list.

"Success means having the courage, the determination and the will to become the person you believe you were meant to be," said George A. Sheehan, a 20th Century athlete, track star and physician.

Consider How Much To Pay Your Ghostwriter

Cost-conscious people might wonder how much they should pay their ghost-writer. While such fees might seem a mystery to some, the answers are easy to locate.

To find the average rates that you should pay to writers, simply visit your local library, mainstream bookstore or go to Amazon.com. There, you should review or order the latest edition of the annual "Writers Market," published by Writers Digest Books.

This publication is considered the "bible" within the book publishing and writing industries. Near the front of the book, which has more than

1,100 pages if you get the recommended "deluxe edition," you'll find the writers' rate chart.

These listings feature the average posted, industry-accepted rates that an experienced ghostwriter should receive. In the "book publishing" section of the rate chart, look for the "as-told-to" and "no-credit" rates that experienced ghostwriters earn.

There, you'll find the "top rate," the "average rate," and the "lowest acceptable rate." What your chosen writer earns depends on his track record and experience. Wayne, for instance, normally commands the "top rate," but he is sometimes willing to accept the average rate if your story, history or philosophy warrant recognition.

In addition to the listed up-front fees, you likely will also need to consider giving the ghostwriter a percentage of the total royalties that you'll earn from your book. A ghostwriter with a highly successful track record likely would require and deserve such compensation.

Decision: A Large Book or a Small Book

Some cash-strapped individuals and even numerous celebrities might entertain the notion of producing a small book rather than a sizable publication in order to save money.

Cramming reams of information into a small space in an energized, breezy and readable manner takes many hours of intense research and vastly superior cogitative abilities.

While at first glance such an option might seem admirable or advisable, we strongly recommend using caution.

You see, as strange as this might sound at first glance, a small, concise and tightly written book is actually much more difficult to compose than wordy, sprawling prose—at least as a general rule or in most cases at least.

Thus, if you tell your ghostwriter that "I only want a small book so that I can limit costs," don't be surprised if this professional's rate increases. Cramming reams of information into a small space in an energized, breezy and readable manner takes many hours of intense research and vastly superior cogitative abilities. Only the best, most-skilled writers can do this in a salable manner that consumers would eagerly buy.

One of the great heroes of modern journalism, "USA Today" founder Al Neuharth, has suggested in his popular weekly "Plain Talk" column that his key advice for writers and on-air communicators is: "Avoid long-winded longwindedness."

Neuharth mentions a book that he says "tells us how to get our personal and professional messages out simply and short." A column by Neuharth describes a unique, must-read book: "Microstyle: The Art of Writing Little," by Christopher Johnson and published by W.W. Norton.

"Johnson points out that nearly all of us are communicators now," Neuharth's column said. "We so-called professionals in print or on the air are far outnumbered by you others who mostly use the Web to get your thoughts out. You do it pretty well. But Johnson's microstyle offers both groups really good advice for better messaging in two key chapters:

1. Be clear and short
2. Give it rhythm

From our view, unless you're a seasoned, naturally talented author, such concise, compelling and succinct communication requires a seasoned professional.

From our view, unless you're a seasoned, naturally talented author, such concise, compelling and succinct communication requires a seasoned professional.

Chapter
6

Should You Self-Publish or Seek a Mainstream Printer?

Once you've decided to write a book, and preferably hired a ghostwriter, you'll need to make an essential first-step decision: Should you self-publish, or seek the services of a large publishing house?

Both negative and positive attributes glisten here. After closely following the industry for years, we strongly recommend the self-publishing route, particularly for aspiring authors who lack big-name celebrity status.

The huge mainstream publishing houses often offer authors miniscule percentages of gross revenues, usually from a paltry 5 percent to 15 percent at most. This compares to 30 percent or even much more for easy-to-use on-demand self publishing services.

The greedy, corporate-minded large publishing houses also have been known to creatively fail to mention to first-time or novice authors that they must work extensively to help promote their books.

Self-published authors sometimes discover that they must undertake similar responsibilities anyway. Invariably, many of these writers end up asking themselves: "Why should I bust my butt to earn money for a huge, selfish company—when I could do precisely the same thing and get most of the profits myself?"

Desperate to downplay such assumptions, the big publishers' representatives might argue that those conglomerates boast multi-million-dollar budgets. Such funds sometimes go toward advertising and wide-scale promotion. For the most part, the vast majority of self-published authors lack such monetary firepower.

Compounding this situation, these conglomerates sometimes offer "big-money" advances, occasionally to the tune of hundreds of thousands of dollars or even millions. Such pitches usually go only to mega-popular celebrities who can brag that "I'm a household name," or authors who already boast a super-successful track record.

"Sooner or later, those who win are those who think they can," said Richard Bach, a best-selling American author of such popular 1970s books as "Jonathan Livingston Seagull," hailed by some fans as a hallmark for the ultimate power of positive thinking.

"Why should I bust my butt to earn money for a huge, selfish company— when I could do precisely the same thing and get most of the profits myself?"

The key to success here hinges on knowing where to go to get your book written, designed and listed within an automatic publishing system.

Position Yourself as a Champion

Only a miniscule percentage of Americans fall within the mega-celebrity category that commands big-money book advances.

Yet thanks to low-cost instant self-publishing systems available today, almost everyone can jump into the big leagues of publishing within the matter of a few months—or even mere weeks.

Yes, as unbelievable as this might sound, it's true. We're among a handful of U.S. book industry consultants who can literally get your book onto the market within a mere month after you start such a project—or perhaps even less.

The key to success here hinges on knowing where to go to get your book written, designed and listed within an automatic publishing system. The amount of time necessary to get a high-quality book onto the market depends on budgeting and scheduling.

When everything hums with efficient energy and creativity in this regard, within as little as 30 days from now your book could be available on Amazon.com, via every online bookseller and through every bookstore in the USA.

"That's amazing!" Some people might tell us when we first give them this news. "How in the world can I do that? Is it really possible?"

We're happy to respond in the affirmative, especially to clients ready, willing and able to devote the resources and time needed to make this all happen.

The "trick" or "secret" to success here becomes possible thanks to the fact that we hail as highly experienced and creative professionals. We know the right and perfect resources to use for getting such jobs done in a high-quality manner.

"Every mind was made for growth, for knowledge, and its nature is sinned against when it is doomed to ignorance," said William Ellery Channing, a Unitarian preacher in the United States in the early 19th Century.

Understand the Benefits of On-Demand Publishing

Avoid feeling ignorant if you never have heard about the many benefits of on-demand book publishing until now.

These systems cost little or nothing for an author to upload his or her book into an automatic printing and distribution system. This marks a sharp contrast from early in this century when aspiring self-publishers hired standard printers to crank out many hundreds or thousands of books.

Although retaining at least some optimism, some new authors of that era got infected with

This compares to today's high-tech systems which never require self-published authors to purchase massive quantities of their own books.

a growing sense of frustration upon realizing the need to store crates of unsold books in their garages, living rooms or at rented storage units.

This compares to today's high-tech systems which never require self-published authors to purchase massive quantities of their own books. Instead, the printers use digital-based computer technology to print precisely the number of books that buyers order. This eliminates any need for storage, thereby minimizing overall production and distribution costs.

Adding to the firepower, the world's best, most efficient on-demand book publishing systems feature automated online ordering software.

These technologies allow the consumers and bookstores to purchase your book directly from the printing company, which handles the monetary transaction. This eliminates any need for the self-publisher to handle the cumbersome chore of handling direct sales, or managing the flow of money.

"Efficiency is doing things right; effectiveness is doing the right things," said Peter F. Drucker, an influential 20th Century writer and self-described "social-ecologist."

Good News: "Your Check Has Arrived"

Adding a perfect layer of frosting to this proverbial cake, the automated process also allows self-publishers to receive instant monthly royalties—paid in a variety of ways:

Direct deposit: The printing company or processor sends your royalty payments directly into your checking account or your savings account—after your amassed revenues have surpassed a pre-specified minimum, usually about $20.

Paper checks: Rather than getting direct deposits, authors can choose to receive paper checks delivered via snail-mail handled through the U.S. Postal Service.

Distributions: Some on-demand services even pay a variety of authors of a single book, each writer receiving his or her authorized percentage of royalty payments.

Pay levels: Royalty rates get set at pre-designated levels, in some cases generating from around $2.50 to $5.50 per sold or printed "dead-tree" book. Per-book sales royalties can creep lower or go much higher, depending on a variety of factors including the book's size and the specific on-demand service that you've chosen.

These automated systems can potentially add up to huge monthly totals, particularly for celebrity authors or first-time writers who suddenly enjoy a boost in book sales.

Understandably, due to this potential for huge

Per-book sales royalties can creep lower or go much higher, depending on a variety of factors including the book's size and the specific on-demand service that you've chosen.

We fully embrace
the strategies
of such clients,
who choose
to create their
books primarily
as a legacy for
passing on to
their children,
grandchildren and
great-grandkids.

revenues, some big-name personalities seriously consider the self-publication route rather than dealing with huge mainstream publishing firms.

"Civilization and profit go hand-in-hand," said Calvin Coolidge, the 30th President of the United States during the height of the Roaring 1920s economic boom.

Another Option: The No-Profit Route

Determined to shun the limelight and refusing to turn their book projects into grabs for big money, some of our clients choose to publish their own life stories—without putting these memories for sale in the mass international and national markets.

We fully embrace the strategies of such clients, who choose to create their books primarily as a legacy for passing on to their children, grandchildren and great-grandkids.

"The legacy of heroes is the memory of a great name and the inheritance of a great example," said Benjamin Disraeli, a 19th Century British prime minister.

Sure enough, as the giant Baby Boom population reaches maturity well past their 50s, 60s and beyond, we serve increasing numbers of clients eager to chronicle their life experiences before they pass away. A vast majority of these individuals never made a "big name for themselves," and they hope to stay out of the media limelight.

Luckily, the world's best, most efficient on-demand printing services make such projects possible, without offering their books for sale. Lots of these first-time authors become just as excited as those seeking a big-money score.

Imagine the joy and pride we feel, for enabling these senior citizens to leave concise, interesting and enduring legacies for their descendants. If it's true what they say, that a "picture is worth 1,000 words," then a book about your life given to your grandchildren can rival the price of all the stars visible on a crystal clear night in the Milky Way.

"There is a strange charm in the hope of a good legacy that wonderfully reduces the sorrow people otherwise may feel for the death of their relatives and friends," said Miguel de Cervantes Saavedra, a popular 16th Century Spanish novelist and playwright.

Avoid Anyone Who Promises You the Moon

"We never can or would promise you that you'll sell even a single book," we tell each of our clients. "Anyone who insists that you'll make big

If it's true what they say, that a "picture is worth 1,000 words," then a book about your life given to your grandchildren can rival the price of all the stars visible on a crystal clear night in the Milky Way.

From our
view, one of the
most deliberate
"failures" rests
on the shoulders
of anyone who
flat-out refuses to
at least entertain
the possibility of
communicating
his or her own
important
messages to the
world.

bucks or millions of dollars printing a book is only trying to deceive you or themselves as well."

You should run in the opposite direction if anyone insists that you have "the story of a lifetime," or that you're "definitely going to cash in big-time thanks to your story idea or your new-found fame—so, hire me to help you."

With such warnings clearly understood, you also need to keep in mind that hitting the grand slam of a lifetime becomes impossible when you refuse to enter the game.

"Victory is the sweetest when you've known defeat," said Malcolm S. Forbes, a mega-wealthy American publisher and businessman.

Throughout the ages, the world's wisest philosophers, psychologists and experts in the human psyche have told us that virtually every person fails at least in some regard. Indeed, as the age-old saying goes, "we're all only human."

From our view, one of the most deliberate "failures" rests on the shoulders of anyone who flat-out refuses to at least entertain the possibility of communicating his or her own important messages to the world.

Take Decisive Action at the Ideal Time

Careful to remain fully cognizant of the many positive possibilities, you should seize the opportunity to get your book project underway as soon as possible.

"I don't have the time," some people say. "Sure, I have an important story to tell the world, but I don't know how to go about getting my message on paper or onto my computer screen in a cohesive, understandable way."

To such people, we say: "Start writing yourself now, this very day while the proverbial iron is hot, or seek the help of a professional writer and ghostwriter."

Tony Robbins, an internationally acclaimed motivational speaker, has often proclaimed that "where energy goes, energy flows." Well, we could not possibly agree more.

Infant humans learning to walk for the first time need only take their initial few steps, before soon mastering the art of how to walk. Thankfully, the same holds true within the realm of learning the craft of how to write—although the actual fine-tuning often takes many years or even decades.

For those who are unable or unwilling to hire a successful, seasoned ghostwriter, a self-education process sometimes emerges as a positive route.

"I don't have the time," some people say. "Sure, I have an important story to tell the world, but I don't know how to go about getting my message on paper or onto my computer screen in a cohesive, understandable way."

By the middle of June just two months after the disaster began officials had increased those estimates to up to 60,000 barrels per day.

Those who select this path can buy and study books on how to craft the written word, or take creative writing classes at the high school or college level. Many communities boast support groups for aspiring writers who share common goals.

A universally accepted saying passed on for many generations tells us that "by ourselves we can enjoy life, but to really appreciate life we must find companionship." Aspiring writers can put themselves on to such a plateau by essentially "hanging out with their own kind," or "recruiting a so-called hired gun who can handle the bulk of the work for you."

Chapter
7

Understand Basics of
On-Demand Publishing

By now, you fully realize the many positive potential benefits of on-demand publishing. At this juncture, the key to success rests largely on finding, using and benefiting from the ideal services among these options, choosing the service best-suited to fulfill your unique needs.

As highly experienced book industry and marketing professionals, we've learned the many positive and negative "ins and outs" of the numerous options.

As if guinea pigs or scout dogs, we've learned the hard way through our own personal and professional experience. In the process we discovered how to pinpoint the potential pitfalls and the most lucrative possibilities.

In essence, through experience and hard work over many years, as a team our efforts have

Thanks to our hard work, failures and successes, herein you'll find the penultimate strategies necessary to position yourself for great possibilities.

managed to focus on strategies best suited to steer clients toward potential success.

Through the years, we've discovered how to avoid printers that generate substandard materials, service providers that charge too much and even publishing executives who strive to dish out a pile of bull.

Thanks to our hard work, failures and successes, herein you'll find the penultimate strategies necessary to position yourself for great possibilities.

"Continual effort—not strength or intelligence—is the key to unlocking our potential," said Winston Churchill, a 20th Century British prime minister.

Choose the Best On-Demand Service for your Needs

Through the past several years, we've become highly familiar with several of the most popular on-demand publishing services.

Some of the busiest include Lightning Source, Book Surge, Create Space, and Lulu. These have emerged as among the most popular services for authors seeking to position themselves for potential riches or high-quality images—or even both.

Based on experience and extensive research, we can testify that each of these services can boast numerous positive features, although saddled with specific potential soft spots as well.

At the start, we urge extreme caution for anyone venturing into this realm for the first time. Choosing the wrong service can result in poor-quality printing, unnecessary expenses, cumbersome application procedures and unnecessary delays.

A Google search seeking analysis, recommendations and commentary invariably turns up a hodge-podge of confusing results. All these primary services each get a "best" or "worst" rating, depending on which reviews you scour at any given moment.

Here the term "buyer-beware" carries more weight than ever. We can't stress enough that choosing the wrong or least-effective system could severely weaken your overall efforts. Conversely, choosing the best service for your particular needs could work wonders, putting you into the big leagues of book publishing and positioning you for big-bucks potential.

"Luck is what happens when preparation meets opportunity," we've been told, and this assumption reigns supreme when deciding which on-demand printer is best for you.

Here the term "buyer-beware" carries more weight than ever. We can't stress enough that choosing the wrong or least-effective system could severely weaken your overall efforts.

Consider These Vital Factors

Right off the bat, we're universally unable to say with great certainty that any particular on-demand printer universally hails as vastly superior to all others. But based on experience, we can list the most important factors for you to consider. Among them:

Communication: Does the service offer a "real-live" customer service person that you can talk by phone with, or merely a cumbersome Web-based instant messaging service?

Promotional copies: Does a particular company feature the lowest-priced services for acquiring prototype and promotional copies of your book?

Royalties: Which service offers you the highest-percentage royalties, the pay that you earn from the sale of your books?

Ease-of-Use: Is the on-demand service's user Website easier to use, understand and navigate than its competitors?

Sign-up Process: Does the service provide an instant and automatic sign-up process for new authors, or are you required to undergo a cumbersome, extensive and difficult-to-pass joining system?

Competitive: How competitive is each on-demand printer's book pricing system, as compared to other firms within this industry segment?

As you might very well imagine, all these various factors—and many more considerations—become extremely complicated and difficult-to-decipher for novice authors. Thankfully, a handful of seasoned and highly trained industry consultants and experts such as us are able to give expert and timely advice on all these criteria.

"Listen to advice, and accept correction—then, in the end, you will be wise," a centuries-old proverb suggests.

True to form, the various factors within the on-demand publishing world are ever-changing, cyclical and chaotic by their very nature. Thus, we would perform a disservice by making any attempt here to recommend a single service over another in every case.

Since we monitor these services on a regular basis— daily in some instances—we invariably remain positioned at all times to give the most reliable recommendations for any particular week or month.

Since we monitor these services on a regular basis—daily in some instances—we invariably remain positioned at all times to give the most reliable recommendations for any particular week or month.

"Never go it alone, or your project is likely doomed to failure," we tell both long-time and new clients. "We truly care about the people and companies that we work with, and we want our valued clients to enjoy success—to get the

> We even heard of a local politician who paid a vanity press more than $13,000 just to get her book published."

recognition they richly deserve, beyond their wildest dreams."

Avoid Costly Vanity Press Companies

Despite the advent of efficient and low-cost on-demand printers, many aspiring writers and senior citizens eager to leave legacies for their families are unfamiliar with such systems.

Even after the advent and widespread emergence of on-demand printing technology, some ill-informed individuals find themselves magnetized by vanity press publishers.

For the most part, other than for a handful of exceptions, we consider vanity programs as costly, unadvisable and highly inefficient.

"We find it sad when some naïve authors get lured by vanity presses," we tell clients. "As disturbing as this might sound, it's true. We even heard of a local politician who paid a vanity press more than $13,000 just to get her book published."

Such news strikes us as both appalling and disturbing, since most on-demand printers enable writers to set up their books for publication at no cost whatsoever, other than for identification number fees and optional work on design and promotion.

In essence, in many cases at least, a vanity publisher agrees to print a specified number of books before making them available to bookstores. From our perspective, such a process is "old-school" and wasteful, largely because many unnecessary books get printed.

Ultimately, everything comes down to this simple question: "Would you rather spend many thousands of dollars to get a vanity press to print and design your book—or would you rather pay 'zero' and get only the books that are necessary?"

From our perspective, such a process is "oldschool" and wasteful, largely because many unnecessary books get printed.

Chapter
8

Beware of Fly-by-Night
Design Systems

B y now you're probably heard the age-old advice, "Never judge a book by its cover."

Yet our experience shows us that quite the opposite is true. A creative, eye-catching and meaningful book cover can make all the difference in determining whether absolutely no copies of a book sell, or the publication is positioned as a potential blockbuster.

"A sloppy, amateur cover design and a poor layout of the interior text can doom your book project from the start," we warn clients. "Above all else, if you hope for any degree of success, you should demand that your project have compelling professional quality."

This is where extreme danger lurks at seemingly every corner. Even some of the most popular on-demand printers offer do-it-yourself systems that enable eager authors to create their own amateurish book covers. Some writers actually fall for this.

Adding fuel to the fire, in an effort to sharply boost their own revenues, just about every on-demand printer offers to create book covers and interior designs for substantial fees.

Once again, over-eager authors face a deadly, costly and tricky trap. Those who swallow such pitches get stuck into an inescapable box. These unlucky individuals get forced to deal with cookie-cutter designers who have never read the book that they're creating.

Matters worsen when you discover that after spending many thousands of dollars, the designer presents you with just one proposed book cover. And you're supposed to "go with" this image, except for just a few slight modifications that you might be allowed to suggest.

Sadly, far too many authors find themselves caught in this net. The situation sometimes gets even stickier when these writers discover all too late that some of these graphic designers have absolutely no solid experience whatsoever— while lacking creativity.

"Just because someone knows how to use a mouse and click or install pre-set images, that doesn't mean they know how to design the best,

"Just because someone knows how to use a mouse and click or install pre-set images, that doesn't mean they know how to design the best, most effective, salable products," Patty sometimes tells clients.

"That's the one!" many clients say. "How in the world did you do this? You've captured the essence of what I hoped to convey."

most effective, salable products," Patty sometimes tells clients. "Every step of the way, you need to go with a highly experienced professional. This added effort could sharply boost your sales and long-term image. And, after all, isn't that what your effort is all about?"

Determined to give the best, highest-quality image services possible, for all of our clients Patty or her staff of seasoned design experts generate a minimum of five or six potential cover layouts for your book. We go the extra mile here only after carefully reading your book, and discussing potential design concepts beforehand.

"That's the one!" many clients say. "How in the world did you do this? You've captured the essence of what I hoped to convey."

Even more important, at no additional cost to clients these images help attract the buyers' eyes when viewed in bookstores. For this reason, Patty's image design firm is called WOW! Design Marketing. To us and for many of our clients, the name fits perfect, since many of our customers instinctively say "Wow" when they first see these images.

Take Great Care in Designing Text

As you might very well imagine, Patty designed the text, layout, design and image of the book you're reading now. Nearly as important as a book's cover in overall function, the text fonts, size and placement within a publication plays a pivotal role.

Disturbingly, all major on-demand printing services feature "free" do-it-yourself layout programs. Even when used by experienced designers, these systems invariably result in cheap-looking, low-quality layouts that make a writer's work appear unprofessional.

"Image is everything," proclaimed a popular 1990s camera product advertising campaign featuring professional tennis star Andre Agassi. This tried-and-true advertising mantra covers everything from TV commercials to display ads and book designs.

Indeed, having a stupid-looking, low-quality image can give a book the appearance of being produced by a non-talented junior high student who rushed a homework assignment. The best way to grab potential buyers by the neck is to use unique, high-quality and cutting-edge designs and layouts.

Even so, major on-demand printers universally realize that a vast majority of authors and marketers who help them lack any inkling of how to generate sizzling designs.

Eager to capitalize and earn big bucks from this wide-open industry loophole, the largest and

The best way to grab potential buyers by the neck is to use unique, high-quality and cutting-edge designs and layouts.

Even worse, due to their intense turn-around requirements and high-volume services for many clients, these designers will never read your book or fully understand its contents.

most productive on-demand printers offer a wide variety of design services—but only in exchange for substantial fees.

All offered at prices that we consider exorbitant, these many features can include: development, shooting and posting of book-promo video trailers, plus the design of media kits, bookmarks, business cards, post cards, posters and "sell sheets" used to collect information from people who buy your book in person.

Using a standard, cookie-cutter graphic design service provided by an on-demand printer could delay your book several weeks or even many months. Requesting just one change to your book's text during the final phase could result in such delays, because turn-around times are a low priority for most on-demand services. Patty can usually make your requested page changes within 72 hours.

Once again, with all these examples, the designer might be an entry-level person with little talent even though you'll be required to fork out big bucks if you choose this option. Even worse, due to their intense turn-around requirements and high-volume services for many clients, these designers will never read your book or fully understand its contents.

By contrast, Patty reads every book for which she designs promotional materials and images—at a higher quality and within a highly competitive fee structure. Ultimately, you should avoid paying cookie-cutter designers exorbitant fees for such materials, and always insist on interacting with a creative person that you have an opportunity to meet or to at least talk with.

All along, keep in mind that such promotional materials remain optional for any book project. You should always approach any high-pressure sales pitches to generate such materials with extreme caution. Just as important, only pursue such public relations efforts if your budget and overall marketing strategy permits.

Demand Expertise, Quality and Experience

Whenever dealing with a graphic designer for your book and any related promotional products, you should always insist that the person fulfill specific qualifications. Among the most important:

Experience: Require that this person has produced a minimum of several dozen designs for high-end corporate and business clients, including lots of book projects.

Drawing: Unlike the bulk of designers who rely solely on inserting pre-formed, pre-set images, your designer should have superior drawing and painting abilities.

History: Your designer should have a minimum

of five years experience, preferably as the top manager or art director of a widely respected company or organization.

Publishing: For best results, you also should seek a designer who has worked for major publishing ventures such as the design of high-circulation magazines.

Awards: Rather than simply getting "stuck" with whatever designer is assigned to you, insist on a professional who has won many top awards within the industry.

Leadership: Besides insisting on all criteria listed above, you also should strive to employ a designer who has owned his or her own successful graphic design company.

Technology: Above all else, make sure that the person remains up-to-date and highly knowledgeable of all the latest and greatest graphic design programs in this highly technical and ever changing publications field.

As you might very well imagine, some of our most loyal clients take great delight in realizing that Patty meets all of the above-listed requirements. A former art director for the California Chamber of Commerce, Patty achieved widespread success throughout the Western United States as one of the world's first graphic designers to incorporate computer technology in her countless award-winning projects.

The lead designer for numerous successful magazines, books, newsletters and Websites, she also hails as a widely acclaimed high-end watercolor portrait artist. Her many commissions include paintings of luxury homes on behalf of various personal estates.

Amazingly, even with all these varied, unique and diverse experiences, she often offers affordable and competitive rates to first-time authors and even for experienced, successful writers. Due to the high demand for Patty's services, she's only able to entertain worthy, socially important or compelling projects.

"Like my husband, Wayne, the ghostwriter, one of my primary life objectives is to help people get the recognition that they richly deserves," Patty sometimes casually tells many of her friends or acquaintances who might ask about her services. "By all means, let's talk about your graphic design needs—because each of us has only one legacy to leave to our world."

Treat Your Book ID Number Like Gold

As you undoubtedly understand by now, we strive to make the entire book production process easy, fun, and value-oriented for all of our clients.

Much of the time, this means taking care of some of the more mundane or intricate chores so that you can concentrate on your primary goal of writing or promotion.

Some on-demand book services provide these numbers for free, as long as you agree to list their company as the "official publisher" or printer.

This is where a vital, necessary step comes to play. All books intended for sale in the general national or international marketplace must have a unique ID code.

Industry experts and even some novices call this an "ISBN," more formally referred to as an International Standard Book Number. Bookstores, online sellers and distributors use these numbers to track sales of a specific book, to record any funds due to the printer and distributor, and ultimately to list any royalty payments due to the writer.

Some on-demand book services provide these numbers for free, as long as you agree to list their company as the "official publisher" or printer.

Rather than take this route, and preferring to set their own course, many first-time writers decide to buy their own ISBN identifiers. Sold only through the Bowker.com service, these cost $125 for a single number, plus an additional $25 for the bar code printed on the back of each book.

Also, for publishers dealing in higher volumes, the ISBN purchase fee is $250 for a bulk package of 10 identifiers at a per-unit rate of $25, or a whopping 1,000 ISBN numbers for $1,000 at a per-unit rate of just $1. Remember, that these fees go directly to Bowker.com, the rates subject to change at any time.

While all this might sound complex or difficult

to put together, our clients have no worries in this regard because we handle all these identifier requirements for them as part of our standard graphic design package.

Use a Unique Name as Your Self-Publisher

Although you technically self-published your book, thanks to today's low-cost start-up fees and on-demand printing there's rarely a need to tell buyers that "I had this published myself," unless you choose to make that declaration.

Many first-time authors quickly discover the positives of starting their own publishing company by creating a formal and legal business entity.

One of the greatest potential benefits from such a strategy emerges when authors use their unique publishing company to legally limit their federal income tax liability. All along, all primary printing, distribution and money management is handled by the on-demand book publisher.

Many years ago when first jumping into this industry, some writers learned the hard way that the IRS slaps people who are self-employed with a much stiffer tax rate than regular wage earners.

In order to legally lower this rate, all you need to do is start a corporation or form a legally licensed

> One of the greatest potential benefits from such a strategy emerges when authors use their unique publishing company to legally limit their federal income tax liability.

Right from the start, new authors need to realize that they must pay federal income taxes on gross income earned from book royalties.

business. Of course, you should consult with your personal tax advisor beforehand to ensure that such a strategy would legally lower your tax liability.

Various Websites offer online application and payment services to start a corporation, limited-liability-company or another type of business entity. In addition, you should check with your state, county or municipal governments to determine what licensing requirements you might need to fulfill.

From our experience, such business start-ups usually take less than a few hours to complete. Of course, only a lawyer can give certified legal advice. Just about everyone experienced in book publishing or general business agrees that forming a corporation or LLC can go a long way toward shielding you personally from potential legal liability—at least in some regards.

In addition, for our most valued customers whose projects seem noteworthy, we sometimes consider the possibility of printing their books within our Fix Bay Inc Publishing division.

Remember to Pay your Taxes

Right from the start, new authors need to realize that they must pay federal income taxes on gross income earned from book royalties.

Especially if your book project steadily emerges as successful, you will need to keep accurate track of your income and legally deductible business expenses.

Unless your book royalties exceed the six-figure mark or the multi-million-dollar milestone, keeping track of your total income should come as a breeze. If you deal solely with a single on-demand printer, during a single calendar year the publisher will send you a maximum of 12 monthly royalty payments.

To ensure that these royalties arrive without a hitch, log in to your unique personal online account at the on-demand printing service. Upon entering your personal "my account" settings area, look for a link that says something like: "Edit Account Settings."

After entering this "edit" section, click on the link that says something like "royalty payment information." When inside this section, input the essential information such as: the name of the person or company that should be paid; whether funds should be paid by paper check or a direct deposit; and your unique taxpayer identification such as a Social Security Number or your company's Employer Identification Number.

In addition, if you have started a company or corporation to receive book royalties, you also need to get a bank account specifically for the purpose of handling those funds. Just like the process of starting a company, this chore often takes less than an hour or two.

In addition, if you have started a company or corporation to receive book royalties, you also need to get a bank account specifically for the purpose of handling those funds.

Those who undertake these simple steps can position themselves for potential financial rewards and long-term savings, especially for book projects that become popular.

"Success is not the key to happiness—happiness is the key to success," said Herman Cain, a former chairman and CEO of Godfather's Pizza. "If you love what you are doing, you will be successful."

Chapter
9

Urgent: Develop an eBook

Online sales of eBooks skyrocketed from 2010 through mid-2011, surpassing the annual purchases of "dead-tree" books for the first time in history.

Wayne envisioned this trend long before expert industry analysts. He created and sold eBooks in the late 1990s, long before big publishers started seizing this opportunity.

"Virtually all serious book writers need to offer both paper books and eBooks," Wayne tells clients. "Without eBooks, you're missing out on huge revenue potential."

The eBook process offers many benefits for authors and buyers. These positive attributes make e-reading software impossible to resist. Among them:

Cost: eBooks are free for authors to produce,

and the purchase costs to consumers are almost always significantly lower than the dead-tree books.

Shipment: Unlike snail-mail shipments of dead-tree books, the delivery of eBooks is instant and "free."

Accessibility: Buyers can view eBooks on their PCs, laptops, cell phones, iPads® and, when sent in a compatible format, via specialized Kindle™ eBook readers.

Timeliness: Rather than wait for the cumbersome, time-consuming printing set-up, authors easily load eBooks online—onto the market within 24 hours.

Pricing: Authors have the option of setting extremely competitive pricing, in some cases sharply enticing potential buyers into making purchases.

Profit: Primary online eBook sales providers offer extremely high profit margins to authors. When a dead-tree book and an eBook under the same title each sell for $10, the writer often earns much more when buyers choose the electronic version.

"Profit is the ignition system of our economic engine," said Charles Sawyer, an American photographer from the late 1800s into the mid-1900s.

Make Kindle™ a High Priority

Electronic-book sales have skyrocketed at Amazon.com since that giant online book-seller launched its original "first-generation" Kindle™ version in November 2007.

According to various published reports, the earliest version of this hand-held or portable device sold for a hefty $399. The per-unit prices subsequently dropped in follow-up versions as Amazon improved the technology.

An "E-Ink Technology Report" said that users gave positive reviews of an improved reader display system in updated versions. Recent prices for Kindles™ ranged from $114 for basic Wi-Fi units, to $139 for 3G Wi-Fi, and $379 for the Kindle™ DX®.

When reviewing these prices you should keep in mind that costs continually fluctuate, just like any hardware product sold in the open marketplace. The best and most reliable place to review current Kindle™ prices is to visit Amazon.com.

As specified groups, consumers and authors each have specific considerations to consider when deciding to enter the Kindle™ marketplace. Among primary considerations:

Review Consumer Benefits

Is the expense of purchasing such units justifiable in the long-run?

When reviewing these prices you should keep in mind that costs continually fluctuate, just like any hardware product sold in the open marketplace.

"As either a consumer or an author, you need to enter this realm as soon as you can," Patty casually tells some of her many friends.

Well, for steadily increasing numbers of consumers the choice here is definitely "yes."

Besides eliminating the need for snail-mail expenses, avid book readers no longer need to fill rooms and shelves full of paper books. Each Kindle™ is designed to store up to 3,500 books.

Also, think of the many cost benefits, environmental savings and the elimination of certain home clean-up chores.

Add to this the numerous other positive Kindle™ features that Amazon.com touts on its Website. Software benefits range from a no-glare in bright sunlight, batteries that last at least two months before recharging, built-in Wi-Fi, 20 percent faster page turns, a "new sleek design," and new enhanced .PDF readers.

Also, determined to spread far and wide into the digital realm preferred by growing numbers of consumers, Kindle™ software is now compatible with a wide variety of platforms and devices. These include everything from Androids™ and the Windows® Phone 7™ to Microsoft Windows™, Mac OS X™, BlackBerry™ and others. Downloading time on Kindles™ and other devices can be done in as little as 60 seconds.

"As either a consumer or an author, you need to enter this realm as soon as you can," Patty casually tells some of her many friends. "In today's super-fast information age, those lacking such technology stand to miss out on vital data necessary to get jobs or educations. For many, the entertainment from reading is just as important."

High Demand Generates Heated Competition

To put this trend into clear perspective, consider the fact that the Alexa ranking lists Amazon.com as the USA's fifth busiest Website and the 17th most popular Web page in the world. This signals that demand for books and unique information sizzles, while tens of millions of Web pages clog the Internet. (Amazon.com offers numerous non-book products as well.)

Adding fuel to the fire, Alexa ranks the popular Barnes and Noble bookseller Web site as the 166th most popular Web page in the United States.

Seeking to benefit from its lofty position, Barnes and Noble's Web site also offers a unique, proprietary e-reader hardware.

Via its primary sites at BN.com and BarnesAndNoble.com, this vendor sells the increasingly popular Nook Readers Tablet hardware. While prices remain subject to change, B&N recently listed $249 as the per-unit cost.

Besides providing the ability to read eBooks, Nook Reader devices enable users to enjoy newspapers, magazines such as "People," and interactive

Adding fuel to the fire, Alexa ranks the popular Barnes and Noble bookseller Web site as the 166th most popular Web page in the United States.

Serious authors eager to profit also need to position themselves onto the SmashWords™ eBook publication and sales line.

children's games. Popular, easy-to-use apps also provide platforms for games, music and email access.

While we lack direct experience with the Nook product, judging by various reviews and media reports, this device stands tall within the industry—giving Amazon a "run for its money."

These factors serve as among primary reasons why every author should strive to make his "dead-tree" products and eBooks available for purchase in as many venues as possible.

Get Listed on SmashWords™

Serious authors eager to profit also need to position themselves onto the SmashWords™ eBook publication and sales line.

SmashWords™ eBooks are increasingly popular among users of iPads™ made by Apple®. Eager and highly motivated to remain on a competitive playing field with Amazon.com, SmashWords™ is offered by leading retailers or software distributors such as Barnes & Noble®, Sony® and Kobo®.

This highly competitive and steadily diversifying system is going head-to-head with Amazon's Kindle™ in a variety of easy-to-download and highly readable formats.

In addition, SmashWords™ enters the

marketplace via multiple platforms including Aldiko™ and Stanza™.

So, rather than miss out on any potential sales, we strongly recommend to all of our authors that they get all their books formatted and listed for sale simultaneously via both the Kindle™ commercial channel and the SmashWords™ line of sales venues. Among primary reasons:

Free entry: Amazon.com and SmashWords™ never charge authors for uploading and offering eBooks.

Diversify: Any author who avoids entering either or both of these primary eBook markets limits his or her income potential, while lessening choices consumers have.

Market saturation: By getting listed in as many unique markets as possible, authors increase chances that consumers will "stumble upon" or discover their books.

Legitimacy: When offering or featuring a book in all venues, an author increases the likelihood of becoming "legitimized" in the consumer mindset.

In summary, if you're serious about being an author and want to increase your project's revenue potential, by all means choose to get listed everywhere possible.

Authors who attempt to create acceptable e-reader file formats before loading those eBooks on their own risk major hassles if something goes wrong.

Conquer any Formatting Challenges

Although Kindle™ and SmashWords™ impose no charge on authors to upload their books in the sellers' marketplace, the process can emerge as cumbersome.

The hassles develop because authors must first convert standard Word™ programs of their book text into strange, HTML-based formats. This process often becomes difficult if not impossible for someone who has never performed such a transition. Compounding matters, Apple™ computer users must format eBooks on other computers, standard PCs; standard Apple™ systems are not compatible with Word™.

Adding to the potential confusion, conducting a Google™ search on "how to create Kindle™ books" offers a vast array of confusing, difficult-to-decipher suggestions.

"Confusion is the welcome mat at the door of creativity," said Michael J. Gelb, who has been described as the "world's leading authority on the application of genius-thinking."

Authors who attempt to create acceptable e-reader file formats before loading those eBooks on their own risk major hassles if something goes wrong. SmashWords™ bans any user that attempts to reload a file twice after initially making a mistake. And, anyone who loads an unintentionally garbled file into Kindle™ risks angering buyers.

As a result, we urge authors to enlist the services of experienced eBook developers such as us, or to hire only recommended services found online to handle these vital chores.

Scour the Web for eBook Venues

Dozens or possibly hundreds of eBook sales venues offer authors sales opportunities. Never overlook this factor, since greater exposure can result in improved sales.

Rather than rest on his or her laurels after their books get offered in all primary markets, authors should spend several weeks signing up with new sales vendors. Among tactics:

Daily: Working daily for at least two weeks to a month, scour the Net searching Google for the term "eBook sellers."

Join: Spend from 10 minutes to 15 minutes daily to complete registration forms at an individual site, before uploading your eBook to offer it for consumers at that venue.

Diversity: After at least two weeks of these easy-to-implement tasks, you'll discover that your eBook is now offered on at least 14 separate venues.

Payoff: The potential payoff could very well come after several months, when these various

Dozens or possibly hundreds of eBook sales venues offer authors sales opportunities. Never overlook this factor, since greater exposure can result in improved sales.

venues start sending you royalty checks if and when sales click into gear.

In addition, some eBook vendors reportedly offer certain electronic publications at rock-bottom rates. Thus, authors should avoid offering their eBooks at services that would eliminate royalties.

"Admire a small ship, but put your freight in a large one. For the larger the load, the greater will be the profit upon profit," said Hesiod, a Greek oral poet in the 7th Century before Christ.

Make Your First Chapter Sizzle

For many generations experienced and successful authors have insisted that all sections of an entire book should shine, particularly the first chapter.

Such suggestions now hold more weight than ever due to the advent of digital e-reader technology. You see, some online booksellers such as Amazon offer potential eBook buyers the chance to read the first chapter of a potential purchase for free. This way the Kindle™ user can decide to go ahead with the final purchase decision.

"Write without pay until someone offers you pay," said Mark Twain, the legendary 19th Century American humorist and classic writer.

In essence, this technology enables potential online buyers the opportunity to browse through the material at least for awhile before making a purchase decision, just like such consumers do at standard brick-and-mortar bookstores.

More than ever before, new or experienced authors need to push much of their energy toward the beginning of every book—to snare the reader with a large, pointy, inescapable literary hook. Think of this as if fishing in a pond filled with cash.

More than ever before, new or experienced authors need to push much of their energy toward the beginning of every book.

Chapter
10

Delve into Marketing and Promotion

Successfully marketing your book to boost sales, solidify your image and position yourself for future successful projects takes commitment, vigilance and focused effort.

Remember, from the start before writing began you conducted research to determine your project's target market.

Then, during the writing phase, the primary chore involved listing the how-to information, historical data or story-line that your most likely potential buyers crave.

Upon completing the writing and publishing phase, the time arrives where you can tell your most likely buyers about your book. Yet you should avoid assuming that everyone will rush out to buy the publication just because you say that it exists.

Along the way, you also should keep in mind the fact that everyone has his or her own life to live, and virtually all of us are bombarded with countless "buy-this" ads daily.

Yet by answering the question "how do I sell this book" even before writing begins, you've already gone a long way toward striving to meet the needs of your most likely buyers.

Nonetheless, as you might very imagine, the question of how best to market a book remains a huge topic in today's highly competitive market. The same challenges face highly experienced and keenly skilled authors and publishers.

Herein you should remember the primary "trick," ensuring that your book is unique, fits a niche from which people will want to buy, and also provides fixes to problems that people experience in today's busy world.

"For every sale you miss because you're too enthusiastic, you will miss a hundred because you're not enthusiastic enough," said Zig Zigler, a successful American motivational speaker, author and salesman.

Study Today's Market

We've already said this, but cannot possibly stress these factors enough: Barring a twist of positive fate or a stroke of unexpected luck, the only way that your book will emerge as a runaway success is by first analyzing your market of potential buyers—before addressing the critical and necessary question of why books sell.

Besides featuring an entertaining story or fixing unique problems, purchases can click into full gear if a book is deemed the unique "first-of-its-kind," features writing by a celebrity or when sales suddenly take off due to positive word-of-mouth.

Your goal should always be to ignite positive, value-oriented buzz for your book—even if the content becomes highly controversial or a matter of intense public debate. In fact, in many instances, the more controversy erupts, the better your sales might become.

"The most savage controversies are about matters as to which there is no good evidence either way," said Bertrand Russell, a 20th Century logician and philosopher.

Fully cognizant of the burning need to fulfill unmet public demand for what your book says, prospects need to get your message that this is a "must-read"—no matter how many interviews you give on TV or radio, or how much you spend on advertising.

Above all else, herein rests an essential reason to ensure that your book is a fine-tuned, well-edited, quick, lively, fun or compelling read. Your readers either wants to enjoy a story that generates intense emotion, or to benefit from valuable life-changing information.

Communicate Your Message to the Marketplace

Rather than striving to merely "sell" your book, you need to effectively communicate your general ideas and concepts or theories to those who are most likely to buy.

Every step of the way you'll need to put your message before as many people as possible, specifically to those individuals most likely to have interest in your topic or story genre.

Once you've put these entire segments of our society into your proverbial cross-hairs, let them know how your books entertains, informs or educates people with similar interests.

Also, to boost your credibility and to demonstrate positive results, give real-life, verifiable positive examples of people who have enjoyed or benefited from your book or from the information found only in your manuscript.

"Today you are you, that is truer than true. There is only one alive who is youer than you," said Dr. Seuss, a classic and extremely popular 20th Century children's book author.

Careful to demonstrate your unique attributes and showing confidence, you need to convey your message in a concise and positive manner. Behaving like a wimp or a cowardly lion will get you just one result—weak, lifeless or non-existent book sales.

Everything from the American classic Civil War epic "Gone With the Wind" by Margaret Mitchell to the recent runaway best-seller "The Help" by Kathryn Stockett has gotten numerous unflattering one-star reviews.

Stare Negative Reviews Straight in the Face

Due largely to the advent of blogs where cowardly critics never have to list their true identities, even some of the greatest classics in American literary history have been receiving at least some negative comments online.

Everything from the American classic Civil War epic "Gone With the Wind" by Margaret Mitchell to the recent runaway best-seller "The Help" by Kathryn Stockett has gotten numerous unflattering one-star reviews. As a result, even the world's greatest classics and the most popular novels of all time lack the highest-possible five-star overall reviews at prestigious sites like Amazon.com.

Like this or not, we have emerged into a society where just about everyone thinks of himself or herself as a knowledgeable, highly educated super critic. As a result, some of the greatest American books of all time often fail to receive full five-star reviews at respected online selling venues.

What all this comes down to is the realization that no matter how well-written, entertaining or informative your book is, some people undoubtedly will dislike what you've done or at least issue less-than-favorable comments.

Mindful of such potential pitfalls, always hold your head high and proud, particularly amid the marketing and communication process. After all, keep in mind that by this point you have blossomed into a certified published author, certainly a reason for pride.

Generate a Marketing Plan

We've met some authors who seemingly would rather jump off the top of the Empire State Building than develop and implant a marketing plan for their books.

Yet since the vast majority of our clients have researched and written their books with a targeted market in mind every step of the way, developing such a plan becomes easy.

Your pre-designed marketing strategy should avoid merely saying "buy" the book, but instead emphasize how readers can either benefit from or enjoy your unique story.

Rather than merely issuing a blatant, shameless sales pitch describing where and how to buy, say things like: "Did you know that you can learn to fly an airplane in less than a week," or "In all honesty, we know a woman who laughed so much when she read this story that she literally could not help but pee her pants."

Then, once you pinpoint the type of market to target and fine-tuned your message, take time to determine which types of media can effectively

Yet since the vast majority of our clients have researched and written their books with a targeted market in mind every step of the way, developing such a plan becomes easy.

Set targets on everything from unit sales and total revenues to establishing yourself as an expert, to generating a steadily increasing revenue stream.

reach the right type of prospects in an economical, efficient and effective manner.

For many savvy and experienced marketers, the best, most effective and economical mediums feature social networking—particularly Facebook™ and Twitter™ in hopes of generating positive buzz and excitement.

Easily and Carefully Analyze Results

Take delight in the process, while continually setting measurable goals that you can later analyze. Set targets on everything from unit sales and total revenues to establishing yourself as an expert, to generating a steadily increasing revenue stream. Among the primary tasks that we recommend considering in order to achieve these goals:

Product: Especially for authors who discover they enjoy the writing process, pump a steadily increasing number of books onto the market. Many writers avidly pursue subsequent works, even if their initial books enjoy little or almost no sales. This strategy targets the long-term objective of getting noticed and gradually building fan bases.

Quality: Work to ensure that all of your books sparkle with an aura of high-quality, everything from the enticement of fine writing to the allure of magnetic images.

Fun: Approach every book project as if the work deserves just as much polishing as all your others, a process that can give the soul a new-found energy. This holds true especially when a product blossoms into a one-of-a-kind flower—emanating a pleasant, robust and enticing aroma for the entire world to enjoy.

Read: Study the market to see what works. This means reading or at least reviewing what consumers have to say about the books of other authors in your chosen genre that bombed or skyrocketed into the best-seller range.

Much of the time, you might find yourself surprised to see that mega-popular authors with dozens of books on the marketplace get average 3-star ratings.

Nonetheless, many of these same authors with lackluster overall reader-review scores still generate sizable incomes, thanks primarily to loyal fans coupled with the fact that lots of the writer's works remain available for purchase.

"If you come to fame not understanding who you are, it will define who you are," said Oprah Winfrey, the iconic and mega-popular TV personality.

Set Your Communication Mode

Both little-known and mega-popular authors face the same integral question: "How much time

Approach every book project as if the work deserves just as much polishing as all your others, a process that can give the soul a new-found energy.

should I spend every day communicating with my current or potential readers?"

A dilemma rests at the heart of such queries. Spending too much time blogging, tweeting or posting FaceBook updates might rob an author of necessary time to create other projects or to handle other responsibilities.

Paradoxically, any refusal to participate in such interactions might get you labeled as a "one-shot-wonder" or a recluse unworthy of any attention let alone book sales.

Faced with such a never-ending Catch-22 dilemma, some authors devise methods of cleverly managing their time. Those adopting this tactic regularly and consistently spend 15 minutes to a half hour daily handling as much social communication as they choose.

For many, following such a game-plan clears the rest of the day for a wide variety of other pursuits from work and entertainment to handling life's many mundane but necessary chores.

"A man cannot be comfortable without his own approval," said Mark Twain, the iconic American humorist and writer.

Blessed with super-success, a handful of celebrities and top-selling authors get the benefit of allowing their professional staff members to handle communication and scheduling. Those of us who lack such luxuries can still position ourselves for success, if we focus on doing what matters most and "working smart."

Experience Will Guide You

Every step of the way, feel free to allow your many failures and successes to serve as an essential guide in dictating what to do in continually pursuing achievable goals.

Also, because your project has targeted the most likely "buyers" from the very start, reach out to companies, organizations, clubs or Websites that show interest in the same subject. Offer to speak to their gatherings, post "free" articles for their newsletters, or show up unexpectedly at their major conventions or community events.

"Give them the gravy, tell them lots of things—but hold back the ultimate details, the so-called meat and potatoes from your book," Wayne tells some clients. "Feel free to open up your free-flowing communication. This way, you can position yourself as a valued expert or at least someone people can reach out to for advice."

Feeling that they lack the time to tackle such chores, some authors put links to their blogs within the Amazon.com system. Other writers benefit from an Amazon program that allows authors to post daily updates at that Website.

Offer to speak to their gatherings, post "free" articles for their newsletters, or show up unexpectedly at their major conventions or community events.

> Authors sometimes reap huge rewards when reporters and reviewers post articles about their books in the general news media.

Among numerous other mediums or communication methods that some authors use to announce their projects:

Press releases: Sometimes found at varying sites for "free" or at moderate fees, these can quickly spread the word. Always have a legitimate newsworthy event to disclose. Authors sometimes reap huge rewards when reporters and reviewers post articles about their books in the general news media. A legitimate, timely and important news story can literally generate 100 times more attention than an expensive display advertisement.

Submit articles: Offer to submit articles for free or for a moderate fee to magazines that target your most likely buyers, such as classic automobile magazines geared to people who build old cars that you've written about. To find magazines, newspapers or Websites related to your primary topic, scour the latest annual issue of "Writer's Market."

On-Air Appearances: Getting a live, on-air radio or TV appearance often gets perceived as extremely difficult for anyone other than a celebrity. But you might find yourself surprised to learn that "persistence is the key," especially for morning radio talk shows at hundreds of local radio stations nationwide.

Having a timely, newsworthy or cutting-edge topic for your book can motivate these media personalities to "get the scoop" by featuring a live question-and-answer session with you. For instance, your latest revealing book of never-before-told stories about tornadoes might get extensive media attention amid a bad storm season in the Southeast United States, the region known as "tornado alley." Whenever possible, schedule your book's initial release immediately before or at the onset of a season that your prospects deem critical.

Product or scientific links: Release your book in tandem with the scheduled launch of a company's new product that you describe, or simultaneously as scientists develop essential or critical new technology.

By jumping into the book market as if the first proverbial horse out of the starter's gate, you can position yourself for victory long before your potential competitors even realize the race has begun.

As a result, some savvy authors continually remain on the lookout for fast-turnaround books offered on the market shortly after timely issues emerge—everything from updates on a deadly hurricane to insider details of a sudden, unexpected war.

"No great man ever complains of want of opportunity," said Ralph Waldo Emerson, the famed 19th Century American essayist, lecturer and poet.

> Whenever possible, schedule your book's initial release immediately before or at the onset of a season that your prospects deem critical.

Build Your Website

Generating a compelling and enticing Website can potentially emerge as critical in an author's long-term success, particularly if he or she has numerous publications.

Yet some writers might argue to the contrary, rightfully contending that they prefer to avoid basing their potential sales on "whether someone thinks my site is pretty enough."

While such "no-Website" strategies often emerge as worthy of merit, those who choose to generate a Web page should ensure their sites offer these attributes:

Newsletters: Feature a free, you-can-always-cancel sign-up form that enables current buyers or prospects to receive regularly scheduled email updates.

Blog: Many highly effective sites feature blogs where an author can post regular updates of opinion or new "how-to" information. Persistently adding new features increases the perception that a Web page is cutting-edge, worthy of return visits. Authors should only enact a blog feature if they have the time and commitment to generate updates.

Sales: Feature links to direct sales within the site, or instant access to vendors like Amazon that offer the books.

For many authors who concentrate primarily on their research, writing or "regular jobs," the mere notion of creating a self-promotion Website looms as potentially expensive, time consuming and a possible pull on their psychic and physical energy.

Through the years we have learned that solutions exist. For those who ask, we can recommend a highly skilled, creative and motivated Web designer and software developer who builds and manages stunning, effective sites for reasonable fees.

But only a limited number of qualified applicants can be considered. So, feel free to contact us if you have a proposal.

Authors should only enact a blog feature if they have the time and commitment to generate updates.

Generate Media Platforms

Authors eager to go direct to their most likely market often choose to develop full-fledged media kits. These packets created by image and design experts like Patty feature everything from press releases and sample books to image files that publications can use along with any story or review that they publish about your book.

Remember that some on-demand book services provide press kit development, but for exorbitant fees. Unlike those systems, Patty works directly with authors that we advise. And, remember, she often reads their books before making suggestions about images. Ultimately, the primary targets for

The other game plan, sometimes used along with various strategies, entails "direct marketing" where you send media kits to a broad-base of recipients.

media kits include journalists, book reviewers and operators of Websites—particularly those interested in your project's topic.

Part of this strategy hinges on direct media relations, where you contact virtually every related Website, organization or company likely to show interest.

The other game plan, sometimes used along with various strategies, entails "direct marketing" where you send media kits to a broad-base of recipients. These can include everything from mailing lists of people who belong to an organization interested in your topic, to handing out flyers to people as they leave stores that offer products related to your book's subject.

"There is no scarcity of opportunity to make a living at what you love," said Wayne Dyer, an author, lecturer and self-help advocate.

Try Public Appearances

The most direct way to interact with your likely market hinges on making public appearances at gatherings that such people often attend.

Essentially, in order to sell your book you're first "selling yourself as an author." By attending their functions, you're essentially communicating to the world that you're "one of them," and have something to say that they should consider of great value.

These appearances might range from promotional tours to bookstore events, lunch parties or gatherings in public libraries.

Rather than portraying a stiff, businesslike appearance as if a "super-salesperson," at these casual gatherings you should always strive to come off as just another regular person. Even in today's celebrity-obsessed culture, many consumers become put off by anyone who acts "holier-than-thou," or behaves as if they're difficult to approach.

> Essentially, in order to sell your book you're first "selling yourself as an author."

Remember here that each person has his own unique problems and worries. Nothing will stop a buyer from purchasing your book faster than a sense of uneasiness. So, you need to make your potential buyers feel safe, relaxed and comfortable in your presence.

"Sales are contingent upon the attitude of the salesman—not the attitude of the prospect," said W. Clement Stone, a 20th Century author and founder of Combined Insurance Co.

Chapter
11

Enjoy Leaving Your Legacy

Whether your goal entails leaving a legacy for your descendants or becoming a popular author, you can and should take great pride in your book project every step of the way.

Even if you only end up selling a handful of books, by taking advantage of today's low-cost on-demand publishing systems you can easily leave a solid mark on our world.

Long after you're gone, people from many cultures will have the opportunity to learn or to experience emotion thanks to the books that you leave behind.

As experienced consultants in the writing, book publishing and marketing industries, we feel a great, overriding sense of warm satisfaction. Imagine the sense of pride and joy we experience whenever a first-time author that we have helped receives his or her book for the first time.

When attending their autograph parties, bookstore presentations or various other public appearances, we prefer to sit in the back row.

This seems right and natural. After all, like we tell every client from the very start, "our job is to get you the recognition that you or your family or business rightfully deserve."

About the Authors

Wayne Rollan Melton and Patty Atcheson-Melton are experienced consultants and practitioners of ghost-writing, book publishing, graphic design and marketing. They base their primary business operations in Reno, Nevada, while serving clients nationwide.

Contact Information

Fix Bay Inc Publishing
316 California Ave., Suite 438
Reno, NV 89509
775-786-2386

www.ingramcontent.com/pod-product-compliance
Lightning Source LLC
Chambersburg PA
CBHW050357280326
41933CB00010BA/1493